Martin Nicholson

Towards a Russia of the Regions

Adelphi Paper 330

Oxford University Press, Great Clarendon Street, Oxford OX2 6DP
Oxford New York
Athens Auckland Bangkok Bombay Calcutta Cape Town
Dar es Salaam Delhi Florence Hong Kong Istanbul Karachi
Kuala Lumpur Madras Madrid Melbourne Mexico City
Nairobi Paris Singapore Taipei Tokyo Toronto
and associated companies in
Berlin Ibadan

Oxford is a trade mark of Oxford University Press

Published in the United States
by Oxford University Press Inc., New York

© The International Institute for Strategic Studies 1999

First published September 1999 by **Oxford University Press** for
The International Institute for Strategic Studies
23 Tavistock Street, London WC2E 7NQ

Director John Chipman
Editor Gerald Segal
Assistant Editor Matthew Foley
Project Manager, Design and Production Mark Taylor

British Library Cataloguing in Publication Data
Data available

Library of Congress Cataloguing in Publication Data

ISBN 0-19-922474-9
ISSN 0567-932x

contents

maps & tables

glossary

CIS	Commonwealth of Independent States
CFE	Conventional Armed Forces in Europe
CPRF	Communist Party of the Russian Federation
CWC	Chemical Weapons Convention
EU	European Union
FSB	Federal Security Service
GDP	gross domestic product
GKI	Federal State Property Committee
LDPR	Liberal Democratic Party of Russia
NDR	Our Home is Russia
OECD	Organisation for Economic Cooperation and Development
OSCE	Organisation for Security and Cooperation in Europe
PSA	production-sharing agreement
SEZ	Special Economic Zone
UNDP	UN Development Programme
VAT	value-added tax
VGTRK	All-Russian Broadcasting Company
WMD	weapons of mass destruction

Since the collapse of the Soviet Union in 1991, Russia's state system has been transformed, but the question of how the country should be governed, or indeed whether it is governable at all, remains unanswered. Russia's federal system has evolved through a series of compromises between central government and regional administrations. The constitutional framework is weak and inherently flawed; the balance of political and economic power, while tilting towards the regions, is in flux.

With the exception of conflict in the North Caucasus, the new pattern of relationships between the centre and the regions has emerged through negotiation rather than bloodshed. Despite their separatist rhetoric, regional leaders remain heavily dependent on the centre for funds and political support, and seek international investment, not recognition as independent states. Russia faces no external threats to its integrity, and its security forces do not support separatism. This short-term stability has, however, been bought at the cost of Russia's long-term political and economic health. In the absence of a firm constitutional framework, regional élites and the vested interests that back them have consolidated power, hampering the development of local democracy and frustrating attempts at grass-roots economic reform. The risk is not that Russia will follow the Soviet Union and fragment, but that the state will effectively cease to function as central and regional élites battle for control over the country's dwindling assets.

Relations between the centre and the regions need to be redefined in two key areas. First, a clear and codified system of fiscal relations should be established to encourage the emergence of transparent, money-based regional economies. Second, the piecemeal devolution of political power to the regions should be rationalised within a precise constitutional framework. Little fundamental reform is likely until at least mid-2000, by which time presidential, parliamentary and regional elections will have been held. Fresh mandates should encourage the key players to see that their long-term interests are better served by placing Russia's federal arrangement within a more regulated framework.

Russia, the world's largest country, requires some kind of federal system. Foreign models of devolution in a once-centralised state, such as Germany or Spain, have specific characteristics that make them unsuited to Russian conditions. In trying to build a genuine federation, Russia has therefore embarked on a large-scale experiment. Although the relationship between the centre and the regions has stimulated only sporadic outside interest, it is as important as the other two pillars of post-Soviet reform: the creation of a multiparty electoral system in place of single-party rule; and the development of a market economy in place of state ownership and central planning. Indeed, the right form of devolution is crucial to the success of both projects.

chapter 1

The Making of Today's Russia

The flawed structure of the Russian state is at the root of the difficult economic and political relationship between the centre and the regions. Unlike the US, Russia is not founded on a contract between its components, nor does it have a carefully constructed German-style constitution. It is instead an amalgam of the quasi-federal structure of the Soviet era, and a series of politically expedient compromises struck in the absence of an effective constitutional settlement.

The Soviet Legacy

In Soviet times, the territory that is now the Russian Federation was known as the Russian Soviet Federative Socialist Republic, the largest of the 15 Union Republics comprising the Union of Soviet Socialist Republics. For 70 years, these disparate entities were held together by the Communist Party. By the late 1980s, the bankruptcy of communist ideology had become clear, and latent nationalism resurfaced. On 6 September 1991, the Soviet Union recognised the independence of Estonia, Latvia and Lithuania; on 8 December, Ukraine, Belarus and Russia formally dissociated themselves from the Soviet Union, which ceased to exist on 25 December 1991. The collapse of the Soviet Union transformed its 15 constituent republics into independent states.

For Russia, independence had three main repercussions, all of which have affected the relationship between the centre and the regions. First, independence paradoxically resulted in a *loss* of identity. The country had gradually expanded, through settlement and conquest, to encompass the territory that became the Russian Empire and then, with some adjustments, the Soviet Union. The stripping away of the 14 surrounding Union Republics prompted fears of a remorseless contraction, eventually leaving the country with nothing but the historic Russian homeland centred on Moscow. Russia's new borders have not in fact been challenged and, with the exception of the North Caucasus, are

an underlying sense of insecurity secure. Russia's leaders nonetheless consistently put the preservation of the country's territorial integrity above any other consideration. This underlying sense of insecurity partly explains the centre's concerns about how far power can be devolved to the regions without causing the disintegration of the state itself.

Second, newly independent Russia lacked viable institutions of regional and central government. Successive Soviet leaders, fearful that a strong Russia would challenge the power of the Soviet Union, deliberately sought to keep it weak. Like the other Union Republics, Russia had its own parliament and government; unlike them, however, its state structures were subsumed under those of the Soviet Union. National communist parties provided the sinews of government in all of the Union Republics except Soviet Russia.

Russia's asymmetrical federal structure, created after the 1917 revolution, was a third disadvantage. Under the Soviet Union's nationality based federal structure, Ukrainians, Georgians and other national groups once part of the Russian Empire were brought together in new, proletarian republics. In the same way, Russia's federal arrangement was intended as a showpiece of Bolshevik nationality policy. Three levels of administrative unit were established:

- autonomous republics, which were home to significant national minorities, such as the Tatars and Bashkirs;
- territorially based regions, in which Russians predominated; and
- autonomous regions and districts, which housed smaller ethnic groups such as the Nentsy and Chukchi.

Autonomous regions and districts were administratively subordinate to the territorially based regions within which they were
situated. In turn, these regions had a lower status than the less
numerous autonomous republics, which had their own constitutions
and state structures. However, unlike the Union Republics, the right
of the autonomous republics to secede was never contemplated, still
less written into any of Soviet Russia's constitutions.

As with the Union Republics, Soviet Russia's autonomous
republics initially helped to promote the culture and identities of
national minorities.[1] But their boundaries were also inaccurate and
divisive: the Buryats were divided into three non-contiguous units,
the Buryat Autonomous Republic and the Ust'-Orda and Aga-Buryat
autonomous districts; Bashkirs were outnumbered by Tatars in the
Bashkir Autonomous Republic; and Turkic and Circassian peoples
were artificially combined within the Kabardino-Balkar Autonomous Republic, and the Karachaevo-Cherkess Autonomous
District. For the Volga Germans and the Chechens and other North
Caucasian peoples, their autonomous republics proved no defence
against deportation by Stalin, who suspected these groups of
collaboration during the Second World War. Nor did the republics in
reality enjoy any special advantages over the territorially based
regions, since the Communist Party was represented at the same
level – the *obkom*, or regional party committee – as in 'ordinary'
regions.

Soviet Russia's asymmetrical federal system was thus of little
practical significance until the late 1980s, when the rise of nationalism gave the autonomous republics the opportunity to exploit
their status. In doing so, they became entangled in the struggle
between the Union Republics and the Soviet Union, and between
Russian President Boris Yeltsin and Soviet leader Mikhail
Gorbachev.[2] In 1990, the Union Republics, including Russia, began
unilaterally to upgrade their status, declaring their sovereignty,
claiming possession of the natural resources on their territories and
asserting the primacy of their laws over those of the Soviet Union. In
turn, autonomous republics and districts declared ownership of
their resources and the primacy of their laws over Russia's, in what
became known as the 'parade of sovereignties'.

The Tatar Autonomous Republic had long begrudged its
lower status as against the smaller Union Republics such as Estonia,

which it outweighed in size, population and industrial capacity. When it declared its sovereignty in August 1990, it was acting not against Russia, but against the institutions of Soviet rule.[3] Yeltsin welcomed the development, with his oft-quoted statement, 'Take as

'take as much sovereignty as you can swallow'

much sovereignty as you can swallow'; Gorbachev, on the other hand, played on the aspirations of the autonomous republics in an effort to fragment his rival's power-base in Russia. In July 1991, the autonomous republics were poised to sign Gorbachev's draft Union Treaty, which attempted to preserve the Soviet Union in a looser form. They were to do so in two capacities: as components of Russia; and as constituents of the Soviet Union commensurate with Russia.

The Russian Constitutional Settlement

The attempted coup against Gorbachev in August 1991 precipitated the break-up of the Soviet Union, and the Union Treaty was never signed. Russia's autonomous republics were not, however, prepared to give up their enhanced status. The integrity of the new Russian state was therefore at risk from its inception, and securing it was one of Yeltsin's most pressing tasks. He did so on 31 March 1992, when all but two of Russia's republics and regions – Chechnya and Tatarstan – signed the Federation Treaty.

The treaty comprised three agreements, one for each of the three types of administrative unit inherited from Soviet Russia. It established:

- 20 nationality based republics (increasing to 21 in June 1992, when Ingushetia, a part of the Chechen–Ingush Autonomous Republic, became a republic in its own right);
- 55 territorially based regions (49 *oblasts* and six larger *krais*), plus the cities of Moscow and St Petersburg; and
- ten autonomous districts (*okrugs*) and one autonomous region, the Jewish Autonomous Oblast.

The Federation Treaty was essentially a holding operation. Although it committed the signatories to accepting that they were part of the new Russian state, it also perpetuated the Soviet hierarchical principle in the first constitutional document adopted by the new

Map I *The Components of the Russian Federation*

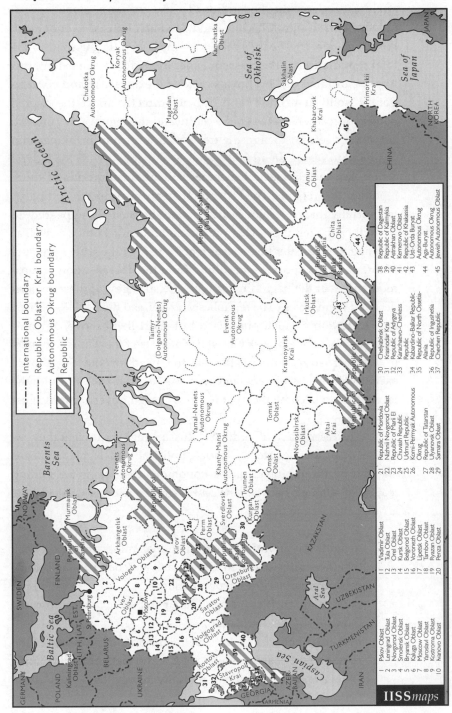

country. While the more separatist-minded republics appended
qualifications to the Federation Treaty, or were given special
inducements to sign, Chechnya and Tatarstan refused to endorse it.
For Chechnya, the treaty's rejection was a step on the road to the
total repudiation of the Russian Federation. To a large extent, this
was the product of Chechnya's historical experience and contem-
porary political turmoil, and did not directly affect the overall
pattern of relations between the centre and the regions. By contrast,
Tatarstan's refusal to sign the treaty was a form of brinkmanship
designed to secure an advantageous arrangement with the federal
centre. As such, it set a benchmark for the aspirations of other
republics and regions. The Federation Treaty also left the 'ordinary',
territorially based regions dissatisfied because it appeared to
strengthen the republics' claims to assets on their territory, as well as
granting them greater financial autonomy. Under the added pressure
of inflation and shortages resulting from the liberalisation of most
retail prices at the beginning of 1992, the strongest of these regions
declared themselves to be republics, and claimed the benefits of their
new status. In a much-publicised but short-lived move, Yeltsin's
home region of Sverdlovsk Oblast declared itself the 'Urals Republic'
in October 1993. Eduard Rossel, the head of the Sverdlovsk
executive, was dismissed, later working his way back through the
legislature to become the region's first elected governor in August
1995.

The resentment of 'ordinary' Russian regions at what they see
as the disproportionate territorial, political and legal privileges
enjoyed by the republics and autonomous districts is an abiding
feature of relations between the centre and the regions. Critics of the
arrangement argue that:

- despite the country's many national minorities, Russians,
  together with Russified Ukrainians and Belorussians, comprise around 82% of the population;
- national minorities living in 'their' republic account for less
  than 10% of the population;
- the titular national group is in the majority in only four of the
  21 nationality based republics – Chechnya, Chuvashia, North
  Ossetia and Tuva – and is a plurality in only three, Kabardino-
  Balkaria, Kalmykia and Tatarstan; and

- the entire population – including Russians – of nationality based administrative units (republics and autonomous districts) accounts for only about 20% of the country's total population.

And yet, critics argue, the republics and autonomous districts cover about half of Russian territory, and enjoy economic privileges and a high degree of political immunity, even when flagrantly breaching the federal constitution. The territorial imbalance is largely the result of the allocation of Russia's huge but thinly populated far north to the Republic of Sakha (Yakutia), which is the size of India, and to seven autonomous districts. But it is true that at least two republics, Tatarstan and Bashkortostan, have negotiated particular financial privileges, while all have enjoyed greater freedom to develop their own sometimes idiosyncratic political systems. Russia's constitutional experts had long recognised the risks of perpetuating the asymmetrical Soviet federal structure. A draft constitution under consideration in the early 1990s would have refashioned the country into some 50 territorial units on the pattern of the German *Länder*, which would have abolished the distinction between the republics and the regions. But the political current was against such a radical solution, and rational proposals were submerged under the developing political struggle between Yeltsin and the Russian parliament.

Yeltsin's victory over the rebellious parliament in October 1993 allowed him to push a hastily drafted constitution through a referendum. It came into force on 12 December 1993, and remains the basic document defining relations between the centre and the regions. As with the Federation Treaty, the constitution's compromises only perpetuated the rivalry between the republics and the regions, because it refined rather than reformed the asymmetrical federal system. Although the constitution maintained that all components of the Russian Federation were equal in their relations with the centre, the republics retained their higher status, with their own constitutions.

The federal constitution also restored a degree of centralisation to the political system. It established the Russian Federation as a three-tier, top-down state (see Figure 1, page 18). At the top are the federal bodies (the president, government and parliament –

Figure 1 *The Structure of the Russian State*

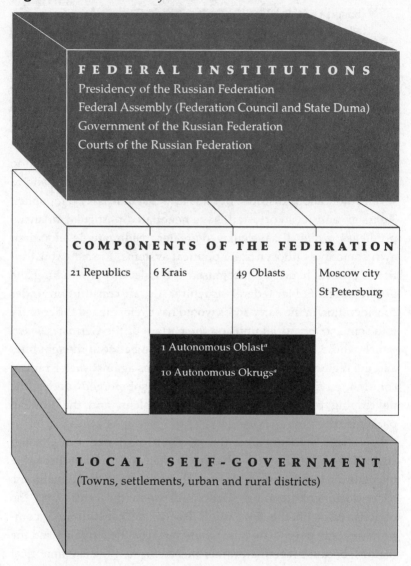

FEDERAL INSTITUTIONS
Presidency of the Russian Federation
Federal Assembly (Federation Council and State Duma)
Government of the Russian Federation
Courts of the Russian Federation

COMPONENTS OF THE FEDERATION

21 Republics 6 Krais 49 Oblasts Moscow city
St Petersburg

1 Autonomous Oblast[a]

10 Autonomous Okrugs[a]

LOCAL SELF-GOVERNMENT
(Towns, settlements, urban and rural districts)

Note [a] These units are both administratively subordinate to the regions
within which they are situated, and constitutionally equal to them

commonly known as 'the centre'). Below them are the federation's 89 components ('the regions', denoted by the deliberately neutral Russian term, *sub'ekt*). The third level comprises local government (the municipalities and below). The constitution's key centralising provisions are:

- the maintenance of a single economic space and a commitment to the free movement of goods, services and financial resources;
- issuing money is the exclusive right of the Central Bank;
- the primacy of federal legislation, and federal control over the judicial system; and
- federal control over foreign and security policies and institutions.

But the constitution is vague over how government is to be exercised in the regions. Such vital questions as the ownership of natural resources and state property, as well as the principles governing taxation, are the joint competence of the federal and regional administrations. Detailed provisions were to be made by federal laws, but scarcely any of these have been adopted. The position of the country's ten autonomous districts and the Jewish Autonomous Oblast in the Far East is particularly ano-

the constitution is vague over how government is to be exercised in the regions

malous. These units are both administratively subordinate to the regions within which they are situated, and constitutionally equal to them. Their status can be changed by federal law, or by bilateral treaty with their parent region.

Under the constitution, the regions are represented in the federal legislature through the Federation Council, the upper house of the Federal Assembly (parliament). In the haste to draft and adopt the constitution, important questions concerning the council's composition and function were left unresolved. All 89 of the federation's components were given the right to two seats and two votes, one from the regional executive, and one from the regional legislature. The council therefore comprises 178 individuals (in practice 176, as Chechnya does not occupy its seats), who adopt decisions by a simple majority vote of the total membership, or by a two-thirds majority in specific cases. This arrangement does not take account of the wide disparity in size and population between the federation's components, nor does it specify how regional representatives should be selected.

Bilateral Deals

By the time the federal constitution came into force, several republics and regions had adopted their own constitutions and charters, under which they gave themselves more rights than the new federal constitution allowed. Tatarstan adopted its own constitution in November 1992, which stated that the republic was merely 'associated' with Russia, rather than a constituent part of the country.[4] Yeltsin and Tatar President Mintimer Shaimiev signed a power-sharing treaty on 15 February 1994, according to which:

> *Tatarstan as a state is united with the Russian Federation by the Constitution of the Russian Federation, by the Constitution of the Republic of Tatarstan and by the treaty on demarcation of subjects of competence and mutual delegation of powers between organs of state power of the Russian Federation and organs of state power of the Republic of Tatarstan.*[5]

A series of agreements was reached on the division of powers at a practical level, the most significant of which covered financial relations. Tatarstan retained the right that it had claimed in 1991–92 to run its own fiscal affairs, while remitting an agreed portion of its tax revenue to the centre. In February 1999, then Russian Minister of Finance Mikhail Zadornov stated that Tatarstan was the only part of the Russian Federation without an office of the Federal Ministry of Finance on its soil; instead, the ministry finances federal institutions in Tatarstan from neighbouring Chuvashia.[6]

The power-sharing treaty with Tatarstan, and a slightly more restrictive one with Bashkortostan in August 1994, set off a competitive bargaining process between the regions and the centre. Treaties were signed with the republics of Sakha (Yakutia), Buryatia and Udmurtia in 1995, increasing the pressure on Yeltsin from the 'ordinary' regions, led by Sverdlovsk. The president, at the time campaigning for re-election, responded generously, and 16 treaties were signed with republics and regions in the first six months of 1996. Not all negotiated power-sharing agreements, and some influential leaders, among them Yegor Stroev (the governor of Orel Oblast and chairman of the Federation Council), opposed them in principle. Nonetheless, 46 had been signed by mid-1999, as well as hundreds of bilateral agreements at lower levels, most of which were kept secret in order to stop the competition for favours from getting out of hand.

The treaties established the practice of individual bargaining, often with Yeltsin himself, as the main vehicle for the conduct of regional relations with the centre. After the initial treaties with Tatarstan and Bashkortostan, these agreements increasingly consisted of regional wish-lists qualified with stipulations that all provisions must accord with federal laws.[7] On 24 June 1999, Yeltsin signed legislation confirming the primacy of the federal constitution and federal laws over individual agreements between the centre and the regions. The law legalised the system of bilateral treaties, but also outlined general principles governing it. In particular, each draft of a treaty must be made available to other components of the federation, allowing them to ensure that their rights are not infringed. Although the law marks progress towards a firm constitutional framework for relations between the centre and the regions, it requires a meticulous review of past legislation and may not be effectively implemented.

The constitutional basis of post-Soviet Russia evolved as a series of compromises reached amid continuous political crisis, and as a result contains two underlying weaknesses. First, the country's asymmetrical structure is unstable because it perpetuates the distortions of the Soviet system. Second, the division of powers between the centre and the regions is vaguely defined. These deficiencies underlie much of the manoeuvring and bargaining that bedevils the economic and political relations between the centre and the regions.

chapter 2

The Economic Dimension

In any federal system, the way in which tax revenue is collected and apportioned is a major aspect of relations between the regions and the centre. In Russia, this issue is especially complex because of the country's varied geography, and because of the distortions caused by the Soviet system and the flawed privatisation process. The regions aim to capitalise on their assets while squeezing as much funding as they can from the centre in the form of transfers, tax breaks and special development programmes. Property and money are thus at the root of the economic strains between the centre and the regions.

The Geopolitical Context

The Russian Federation is the world's largest state by land-mass, with wide variations in geography and climate, ranging from the inhospitable north-east to the temperate south-west. For ideological and political reasons, the Soviet system ignored these natural differences; industries were located where it suited the central planners or those who ran the forced-labour camps, rather than with a view to balanced regional development. Since the social infrastructure developed around factories, there was little scope for its organic growth. Defence enterprises, and sometimes whole towns, were cut off from their surroundings and depended on the central government for food and consumer goods. As a result, few regions emerged from the end of the Soviet era as rounded economic and social units.

Many of the regions that benefited most from the Soviet system – primarily those with a concentration of defence industries and situated far from Russia's European core – have fared worst following the collapse of central planning and financing. The end of Soviet transport subsidies has in particular affected the economies of regions in Siberia and the Russian Far East, while agricultural regions suffer under the legacy of Soviet collectivisation. Others have done better, notably those with access to metals, timber or hydrocarbons that can be sold abroad for hard currency; and 'gateway' or 'nodal' regions, built around large conurbations, with good transport and financial links.

Although the statistical base for calculating the relative prosperity of Russia's regions is undeveloped and no two rankings agree, the following usually figure among the country's top dozen regions:

- the prime 'gateway' regions of Moscow city and Oblast, together with St Petersburg;
- Samara, Nizhnii Novgorod, Perm and Sverdlovsk, all industrial regions with good infrastructure;
- the resource-rich Tatarstan and Bashkortostan, which also have good infrastructure; and
- Krasnoyarsk, Irkutsk and Tyumen.

Tyumen Oblast's vast oil and natural-gas resources are all on the territory of two autonomous districts, Khanty-Mansi and Yamal-Nenets. Both, although administratively subordinate to Tyumen, have claimed their constitutional right to deal directly with the centre, and to enjoy the benefits of their resource wealth. A similar anomaly affects Krasnoyarsk Krai. Norilsk Nikel, the world's largest nickel concern, has its major plant on the territory of the Taimyr Autonomous District within Krasnoyarsk, but the town of Norilsk itself has, since 1943, been directly subordinate to the federal centre.[1] Peculiarities such as these make it more difficult to establish a fair system for collecting and distributing revenues, and complicate the formation of regional identities.

The greatest anomaly of all is the city of Moscow. Although in principle one of Russia's 89 equal components, as the federal capital it is looked upon by the rest of the country with a mix of envy and respect. The city has retained its role as the hub of the state, but now has the added advantage of being the country's financial centre in the new, quasi-market conditions. In 1997, Moscow attracted 78% of all foreign direct investment, and provided 40% of the federal budget's income.[2] Moscow's wealth and power have exacerbated the divide between 'the centre' and 'the periphery' that is one of the barriers to creating a genuine federation. Russian politicians have occasionally suggested that the federal capital should be moved; Novosibirsk, Russia's geographic centre, and Vologda, its historic heart, have been mentioned. In May 1999, moderate Russian politician Vladimir Ryzhkov, the leader of the parliamentary faction of the pro-government political party Our Home is Russia (NDR), argued that the federal capital should be moved from the country's main centre of finance and power. Ryzhkov's suggested location was Velikii Novgorod, the birthplace of Russian republicanism midway between Moscow and St Petersburg.[3]

Despite the prevailing view in the 'ordinary' regions that the republics have gained an unfair advantage through the post-Soviet constitutional settlement, only those republics with resources have been able to benefit economically from their privileged political status. Tatarstan occupies a strategic position across major transport routes, whilst its oil production accounts for 8% of Russia's total. Bashkortostan is a key centre for the chemical and petrochemical industries, and a transit-point for gas and oil pipelines. But most of the other 21 republics remain at the bottom of the prosperity pile. In a 1998 human-development index prepared by the UN Development Programme (UNDP), Bashkortostan and Tatarstan are the only republics to figure among Russia's top ten regions. Republics from the North Caucasus and southern Siberia, along with the Jewish Autonomous Oblast, account for nine of the bottom ten (see Table 1, page 26).[4]

Regional Elites and Property Relations

In the Soviet Union, natural resources and property of any significance were owned by the state in the name of 'the people'. Other than in wartime, centralised economic planning and management was never especially practical, and it became ever less so as the economy increased in size and complexity. In parallel with the planned economy, informal networks developed between

Table 1 *Russia's Prosperity, by Region*

	Per-capita gross regional product (US$)	Life expectancy (years)	Proportion of students (%)[b]	Human Development Index[a]
Top ten regions				
Moscow	6,798	67.5	84.7	0.867
Republic of Tatarstan	7,632	68.2	71.5	0.857
St Petersburg	5,005	68.4	78.2	0.852
Republic of Bashkortostan	5,845	67.2	73.3	0.851
Nizhnii Novgorod Oblast	5,314	66.5	76.0	0.849
Lipetsk Oblast	5,320	67.4	70.4	0.847
Tyumen Oblast	13,122	65.3	66.5	0.841
Samara Oblast	6,184	66.1	68.2	0.840
Perm Oblast	5,542	64.5	67.1	0.828
Tomsk Oblast	5,200	64.3	67.7	0.826
Bottom ten regions				
Republic of Marii El	2,018	67.1	67.9	0.648
Republic of Adygeya	1,907	67.8	69.6	0.647
Republic of North Ossetia	1,724	67.3	78.0	0.642
Republic of Kalmykia	1,545	66.7	74.8	0.624
Chita Oblast	1,974	63.1	63.9	0.618
Republic of Altai	1,961	62.4	68.0	0.618
Republic of Dagestan	1,251	70.3	66.7	0.616
Jewish Autonomous Oblast	1,829	61.7	65.3	0.603
Republic of Ingushetia	1,078	71.5	51.0	0.595
Republic of Tuva	1,029	55.4	67.0	0.520

Notes [a] As computed by the UN Development Programme (UNDP), the Human Development Index is based on three indicators: per-capita gross regional product; life expectancy; and educational attainment. All data are for 1996
[b] Percentages denote the proportion of the regional population between the ages of seven and 24 attending an educational institution

Source *Human Development Report 1998, Russian Federation* (Moscow: UNDP, 1998), pp. 77, 78

enterprises and their directing ministry in Moscow; between enterprises located near each other but reporting to different ministries; and between all of these and the regional committee of the Communist Party and the regional Soviet (the local legislature). Only the local party authorities had any kind of overview of the economic situation in their areas, and acted as links between economic entities to deal with scarcities and bottlenecks.[5] In a short-lived reform between 1957 and 1962, Soviet leader Nikita Khrushchev replaced the Moscow-based industrial ministries with Regional Economic Councils, whose boundaries coincided with those of the *oblasts*. The local party leader assumed the authority of a minister, dealing with all the large-scale industry in his region.[6] Although the reform recognised that the economy could no longer be run effectively from the centre, it was abandoned because it threatened to give too much power to the regions. In another of the Soviet system's peculiarities, major enterprises assumed the local authorities' responsibilities for providing housing, leisure and transport facilities for their employees, cementing the ties between local party authorities and industrial leaders. As a result, 'regional élites' – a close fraternity of local political, industrial and financial leaders – had become deeply entrenched by the end of the Soviet period. Despite the temporary emergence of democratic politicians in the regions, particularly in urban legislatures from the start of free elections in 1990, these élites maintained their cohesion after the Soviet system's collapse, and tended to assimilate, rather than challenge, new business and criminal interests. Under Yeltsin, an estimated 82% of the former Soviet élite in the regions retained positions of influence, as did 75% in the centre.[7]

The 'shock-therapy' economic reforms which began in 1992 did not loosen the hold of regional élites on what they increasingly saw as 'their' economies. Under the partial price liberalisation of January 1992, regional leaders were permitted to keep some controls in their own jurisdictions. In a celebrated case, the governor and former Communist Party boss of Ulyanovsk Oblast, Yurii Goryachev, maintained the central elements of the socialist economy – low pay and taxation, high social spending, price controls and rationing – in the face of the prevailing free-market ethos. Whether or not these measures were economically prudent, they were popular locally, and Goryachev was re-elected in December 1996.[8] In response to the financial crisis of August 1998, prompted by a 30% devaluation of the rouble, Stavropol Krai, Bashkortostan and other regions imposed price controls and restricted the movement of goods.[9] The Republic of Kalmykia temporarily stopped remitting taxes to the centre. The crisis strengthened the regional administrations' hold over local economies at the expense of the centre. Regional banks emerged relatively stronger than local branches of Moscow-based houses because they were less exposed to Moscow's volatile securities market, and had not borrowed heavily abroad.[10] In a bid for greater financial self-sufficiency, Perm, Sverdlovsk, Kemerovo, Irkutsk, Sakha (Yakutia) and Magadan created their own gold and foreign-currency reserves, as they were legally entitled to do.

regional banks were less exposed to Moscow's volatile securities market

The first stage of privatisation, which accompanied price liberalisation, also played into the hands of the regional élites. Small-scale privatisation was devolved to the municipalities. The Federal State Property Committee (GKI) administered large-scale privatisation through its regional branches, which functioned as departments of the regional administrations. This meant that the regional administration was responsible for managing, and in effect owned, property in transition between the state and a new corporate owner, who frequently turned out to be the same Soviet-era director. In July 1996, Yeltsin appointed two former GKI chairmen, Anatolii Chubais and Aleksandr Kazakov, to the President's Administration, where the most important business with the regions was done. Chubais became the administration's head, Kazakov its deputy head responsible for regional affairs. In this way, the personal bonds made between central and regional political élites during the privatisation process became central to the economic relations between the centre and the regions.

Regional leaders consolidated their control over local economies by creating holding companies, which loosely amalgamated a number of enterprises under management boards on which regional authorities were strongly represented. In 1991, then Deputy Moscow Mayor Yurii Luzhkov formed the Sistema Group around his own construction and media interests. Three years later, Yevgenii Nazdratenko, the governor of Primorskii Krai, created the joint-stock company PAKT, which comprises 36 leading regional industrial enterprises, including six defence plants, four fishing and fish-processing companies, and producers of chemicals and electronic circuits.[11] Regional administrations also took shares in enterprises of regional significance, such as the automobile plant AvtoVAZ in Samara Oblast and the Tatarstan oil company Tatneft, in order to ensure that the region's interests were reflected in company policy. Tatar Prime Minister Rustam Minnekhanov is chairman of Tatneft's board. Enterprise directors are commonly members of the regional legislature.

The interests of regional élites frequently obstruct economic reform on the ground. There is often a conflict between the requirement to close an obsolete plant, and the regional leadership's perceived duty to protect the population from the hardship that doing so would cause. Embezzlement can also keep non-performing enterprises open, as regional leaders channel funds out of large concerns in collusion with local business associates. Enterprises that fail to generate profits can settle bills only by barter, promissory notes or tax offsets. For example, if a local enterprise cannot pay for its fuel, then its energy supplier is unable to pay its local taxes in cash. By agreement with the local administration, it might instead supply free fuel to a school or hospital which the administration itself is unable to fund because it has not received any tax payments in cash. The administration may have to accept some construction work *regional élites frequently obstruct economic reform* from a local firm as tax payment, even if its real need is cash to pay teachers. In 1996, regional budgets received on average just 50% of their revenue in real money.[12] Regional élites are deeply involved in the discounts and shady deals that form part of this system.

Most regions depend on the outside world for imports of fuel and raw materials, and for transport and other infrastructure services. They therefore have a symbiotic relationship with the natural monopolies:

- Gazprom, which controls the production, transport and distribution of Russia's natural gas;
- United Energy Systems, a holding company comprising 72 privatised or partly privatised regional power systems

controlling two-thirds of Russia's installed generating capacity;[13] and

- the railway network, which negotiates individually with 79 of the federation's 89 components.

These organisations are quasi-state monopolies, whose loyalties lie ultimately with the centre. They can thus be used by the federal authorities as indirect instruments to coerce the regions. But they also operate at regional level, where they both reflect and contribute to the non-payment cycle. Gazprom, for example, argues that many of its customers unable to settle their gas bills in cash are municipalities or state concerns, including the military. Cutting off supplies to them might have serious political and economic consequences. Gazprom therefore invariably becomes involved in the barter and special agreements that keep local economies staggering on, insolvent and opaque.

In April 1998, Chubais became chief executive of the electricity provider United Energy Systems, and began trying to rationalise the energy network. The difficulties that he has faced show how the regions can resist attempts to impose market mechanisms. Many regional energy providers operate as local monopolies, and continue the Soviet system of cross-subsidisation, where industry subsidises private electricity consumers. Approximately one-third of Russia's power is distributed in regions where industry pays at least three times more than residential customers.[14] Regional governors defend the current system, since it gives them some control over local utilities. Abandoning it would cause numerous political problems, including a sharp rise in domestic fuel prices. In May 1998, regional administrations secured the legal right to control over half of the state's 51% shareholding in United Energy Systems.

Regional élites do not, of course, have a free hand in their own territories. Many of the protectionist measures introduced in the wake of the 1998 crisis were sabotaged by retailers who withheld their products from the shops until they were able to charge a realistic price, or by producers bribing the police to allow their goods through regional boundaries. Threats by regional leaders to withhold taxes from the centre are largely bluff, since they do not have the power directly to divert monies collected by federal agencies. Despite claims to be self-sufficient, regional and central economies remain interdependent. In June 1998, insufficient central funds were available to service the regions' internal debts, causing them to default.[15] After the August crisis, international agencies refused to award regions a higher credit rating than the country as a whole.

Krasnoyarsk Governor Aleksandr Lebed's confrontation with Anatolii Bykov, a leading regional businessman with an allegedly criminal past, illustrates the centre's continuing role as a power-broker, if not as a power in its own right. It is also a good example of the imbroglio of politics, business and crime in the regions, and of the constraints on regional leaders' actions. Lebed found himself pitted against Bykov, his erstwhile supporter, shortly after he won Krasnoyarsk's gubernatorial elections in May 1998. Bykov, Chair-man of the Board of Russia's second-largest aluminium factory, Krasnoyarsk Aluminium (KrAZ), appears to have assumed that, in return for his backing, Lebed would support his bid to create a large energy–metallurgical corporation, incorporating KrAZ, the Krasnoy-arsk Coal Mining Company (Krasugol), a federally owned holding company which provides over a quarter of the coal consumed by United Energy Systems, and other local enterprises. Lebed, however, opposed the merger on the grounds that the new corporation would not be paying sufficient tax locally. In response, Bykov tried to gain control of Krasugol, which owed 72 billion roubles to United Energy Systems, by initiating bankruptcy proceedings against the company.

In his battle with Bykov, Lebed called in a task-force from the Ministry of the Interior under Deputy Minister Vladimir Kolesnikov to investigate the finances of KrAZ. Its preliminary findings showed that the privatisation of the company had been carried out illegally, and an arrest warrant was issued against Bykov.[16] Lebed also turned to Chubais to forgive Krasugol's debt. Chubais agreed only on condition that United Energy Systems acquired equity in Krasugol, which Lebed rejected. Finally, the governor persuaded then Minister of Fuel and Power Sergei Generalov to release the necessary funds. On 10 April 1999, Lebed signed an agreement with then Prime Minister Yevgeny Primakov dividing control over Krasugol equally between the Krasnoyarsk authorities and the federal government.

Table 2 *Division of Tax Revenues, 1998*

Tax	Percentage to the centre	Percentage to the region
Excise (energy and imports)	100	0
Value-added tax	75	25
Excise (domestically produced alcohol)	50	50
Profit tax[a]	37	63
Personal income tax	0	100

Note   [a] Regions are permitted to impose a limited surtax, up to a maximum of 9% above the federal tax rate of 13%

Source   Erik Nelson and Al Breach, *Russia: The Federation and Its Subjects – How Much Decentralisation?*, Goldmann Sachs, 30 November 1998, p. S17

Fiscal Federalism

A major cause of the economic and political disputes between the centre and the regions is the lack of an agreed basis for collecting and distributing revenue. The unitary Soviet fiscal system began to unravel in the late 1980s, when the Union Republics claimed the right to raise their own taxes, and remit what they considered appropriate to the federal government. When Russia became

no agreed basis for collecting and distributing revenue

independent, Tatarstan and other leading republics collected their own taxes and transferred a fixed amount, below the national average, to the federal budget. Leading regions such as Sverdlovsk followed suit, while less favoured ones had to introduce a plethora of local taxes to stay afloat.

The central government re-established a measure of control only after Yeltsin reasserted his authority at the end of 1993. However, a federal Tax Code stipulated under the new constitution was derailed by the 1998 crisis; only the first and most general part of this legislation was adopted beforehand, coming into force on 1 January 1999. In the absence of a general taxation law, tax and budgetary relations between the centre and the regions are based on a presidential decree of January 1994, but are subject to constant change. Federal taxes (which are levied on enterprises, not on regions as such) are raised by the centre and collected by federal officials based in the regions. They are shared with the regions in proportions that are decided annually in the budget. The regions are permitted to raise a large number of local taxes, for example on property and land. In 1998, there were four main federal taxes: excise duties on energy and imports, and on domestically produced alcohol; value-added tax (VAT); profit tax; and personal income tax (see Table 2, page 32).

The distribution of these revenues has aroused criticism from the regions on a number of grounds:

- the centre receives the lion's share of the steady, indirect taxes (VAT and excise), while profit and income tax, which are divided in favour of the regions, are cyclical and harder to collect;
- the centre can assign expenditures to the regions without guaranteeing that this spending will be covered by revenue;
- the proportion of taxes remitted to the regions varies from year to year, making financial planning impossible;
- VAT is collected at company head offices, which are often located in Moscow (this is one reason for the capital's disproportionate wealth); and
- the regions' receipt of their share of revenues is delayed because the money travels to the centre before being redistributed to the regions (although this principle can be circumvented in practice by bilateral agreement).

Under the 1994 decree, a proportion of the revenue accruing to the centre (set at 27% in 1995, but reduced to 14% in 1998) would be put into a new Federal Fund for Regional Support. The fund was to be the sole source of regional subsidies, and was intended to reduce economic inequalities and geographic disadvantages. It relied on a complex system of weighting to establish which regions should be in the two categories of 'recipients' ('needy' and 'very needy'), and which in the category of 'donor', which under this scheme received no transfers from the federal budget. The number of donors has varied with changes in the distribution of revenue; in 1999 there were 13.[17] In addition to the obvious candidates – Moscow, St Petersburg and the industrial regions of Samara and Sverdlovsk – donors also include the Khanty-Mansi and Yamal-Nenets autonomous districts.

The regional support system has outlived its usefulness. Calculating the regions' status has become an ever-more complex and obscure process. Since it is based, Soviet-style, on the 'achievements' of the previous year, regions are encouraged to minimise their economic activity, thus qualifying for increased aid. This has caused resentment among the 'donor' regions. The system is also not an accurate indicator of the total flow of money from the centre to the regions since it encompasses only about half of the funds transferred; loans or funds for special projects are not included.[18] Worst of all, from the centre's point of view, transfers are made as lump sums, with no control over how they are spent.

Before the financial and political crisis of August 1998, attempts to reform the system had begun. Prime Minister Sergei Kiriyenko's short-lived government of April–August 1998 embarked on a valiant, if quixotic, effort to fulfil a presidential decree of 5 May 1998 ordering the government to conclude fiscal-reform agreements with all regional authorities. The aim was to make transfers conditional on:

- tax revenue from the regions accruing in real money, and an end to offsets in payments to the centre;
- regions implementing government policies to reduce subsidies for rent and municipal services; and
- no subventions from regional budgets being paid to companies with tax arrears to the federal or regional budget.

Although the fall of Kiriyenko's government killed off this initiative, his successor as prime minister, Primakov, took up where he left off. Primakov's initiative was worked on by many of the same officials who had produced Kiriyenko's. It involved making the regions responsible for collecting revenues by instituting a new sales tax, a

pre-sales tax on local traders with inadequate accounting procedures, and levying VAT on large corporations at the place where
their main economic activity took place, rather than where they were
registered. By mid-1999, more than 40 regions had reluctantly
imposed the unpopular sales tax. But regional leaders such as
Ingush President Ruslan Aushev also
argued that, if they were to be made *the centre needs to*
responsible for tax gathering, they *negotiate a new tax code*
should be allowed to keep what they *with regional leaders*
collected and transfer a fixed portion
to the centre – the so-called 'single-channel' tax. Since the unilateral
institution of this revenue-collection system by Soviet Russia and
other Union Republics contributed to the break-up of the Soviet
Union, the central government will not contemplate its
reintroduction. Problems will therefore persist until the centre can
muster sufficient strength and sense of purpose to negotiate the
detailed chapters of a new tax code with regional leaders.

From heady beginnings, when they acquired control over the
wealth-creating assets of the former Soviet Union, regional leaders
have become locked into an economic system that is neither
'socialist' nor 'capitalist', but a battle of vested interests in which
normal economic indicators, including money, play little part. Most
regions remain dependent on the centre, despite claims to self-
sufficiency following the 1998 crisis. The extent to which they can
maximise their assets or make good their threats of unilateral action
depends on their political strength relative to the centre, and on their
capacity to exert collective political pressure.

chapter 3

The Political Dimension

Under the centralised Soviet regime, the political fate of Communist Party leaders in the regions hinged on decisions made in Moscow. The ultimate prize for an aspiring regional politician was a transfer to a significant post in the centre – the road taken by both Gorbachev and Yeltsin, former Communist Party bosses in Stavropol Krai and Sverdlovsk Oblast respectively. The general weakening of the centre's authority following the collapse of the party structure in 1991 made a political career in the regions more attractive for its own sake, rather than as a stepping-stone to national power. Popular elections, which have no precedent in Soviet or earlier Russian history, have given regional leaders a solid political base and considerable room for manoeuvre.

Power to the Regions: The Election of Governors

With the demise of the Communist Party, leadership in the regions devolved to the chairmen of the executive committees of the regional Soviets, the largely powerless regional legislatures. Following his battle with the national parliament in 1993, however, Yeltsin dissolved the Soviets and appointed heads of administration to run the territorially based regions. Yeltsin did not intend these governors (*gubernatory*), as they became known, to be popularly elected. He had endorsed the principle early in 1991 in order to circumvent the regional Soviets, but reversed his decision later that year when it became clear that many of his opponents would probably win if elections were held. The events of 1993, when a number of governors sided with his parliamentary opponents, only strengthened Yeltsin's resolve and, in a decree of October 1994, he reasserted his right to nominate and dismiss governors.[1] This did not contravene the constitution which, although it endorses the principle of elections, does not provide for the election of the heads of regional executives. Instead, it declares that the 'federal bodies of executive power and bodies of executive power of the components of the Russian Federation comprise a single system of executive power in the Russian Federation'. This provision was frequently cited by officials in Yeltsin's administration, and later also by Primakov as prime minister, to argue for a top-down government structure, rather than popularly elected governors.

Three political considerations forced Yeltsin gradually to concede. First, all but three of the nationality based republics had held leadership elections between 1991 and 1995, and the centre had tacitly accepted their right to organise their own internal politics. Second, some of Yeltsin's loyal political appointees, among them then Governor Boris Nemtsov of Nizhnii Novgorod Oblast, argued that, just as the president's authority depended on a popular mandate, so should theirs if reforms were to continue. Third, and decisively, in order to secure the type of Federation Council that he wanted, Yeltsin was compelled to agree at the end of 1995 to the popular election of governors where it had not already taken place. Yeltsin had wanted the regions to be represented in the council by their executive and legislative leaders *ex officio*. This was opposed by the Duma, the new parliament's lower house, because it would have meant that almost half of the council's members would be Yeltsin appointees. As a compromise, it was agreed that the council should comprise the heads of the two branches of power *ex officio*, but that the leaders of the regional executives should first have been elected locally, as those of the legislatures already were. Between September 1996 and March 1997, 46 regions held their first-ever elections for governor.

Initially, both Yeltsin and his communist opponents saw these polls as a continuation of the battle for the presidency between Yeltsin and communist leader Gennadii Zyuganov in July 1996. On 1 September 1996, a pro-Yeltsin politician, Dmitrii Ayatskov, won a decisive victory in the first of these elections, held in the hitherto pro-communist Saratov Oblast. As the polls proceeded, it became clear that supporting the president did not always guarantee victory. However, Yeltsin's ideological opponents failed to capitalise on their successes. They did best in the poorest regions, which depended the most on support from the centre. Their leaders could not therefore afford a confrontation with the federal authorities if they were to lobby successfully for special regional programmes and federal off-budget funds. They thus pioneered a new, non-ideological style of politics, advertising themselves as *khozyaistvenniki* – 'hands-on managers' – concerned with the welfare of their provinces, rather than with political battles in distant Moscow. As a result, the new regional leaderships have emerged as a stabilising influence when political crises, such as Yeltsin's confrontations with the parliament, have broken.

regional leaderships have emerged as a stabilising influence

Although democratically elected, regional leaders have found it difficult to reconcile their new power with the niceties of democratic politics, tending instead to interpret their mandate as giving them an exclusive hold on power in their region. They aim to obtain the support of, or neutralise, the regional legislature, which is elected separately from the governor and whose laws set the framework for a significant portion of a region's political and economic life. With some exceptions, notably St Petersburg and Primorskii Krai, governors have created their own formal or informal 'parties of power' that control the legislature.

Governors also aim to control the local media. In the post-Soviet economic turmoil, the reach of the national media has been severely curtailed. Only one quasi-state television channel, ORT, the successor of the Soviet state broadcaster, and one newspaper, the official *Rossiiskaya Gazeta*, regularly reach all of the country's provinces. Local news channels, on the other hand, have proliferated. Regional leaders have used a variety of methods – many of them indirect, deriving for example from their control of paper supplies – to suppress dissenting voices. In an extreme case, which aroused national concern, Larisa Yudina, an independent journalist and persistent critic of Kalmyk President Kirsan Ilyumzhinov, was killed in June 1998. Two members of the president's entourage were subsequently charged with her murder.[2] The battle for media control intensified within regions, and between the regions and the centre, in the run-up to national and regional elections in 1999–2000. In May 1998, Yeltsin issued a decree turning state-owned regional broadcasting companies, which were effectively under the control of the regional authorities, into affiliates of the official central channel, the All-Russian Broadcasting Company (VGTRK). The decree provoked a number of confrontations between central and regional authorities. In December 1998, Lebed appointed one of his allies, Oleg Nelzin, as head of the Krasnoyarsk State Television and Radio Company in a bid to prevent its transfer to federal control. Lebed signed a compromise agreement in February 1999 with Mikhail Shvydkoi, the chairman of VGTRK, under which the national network regained control of Krasnoyarsk's television company in exchange for guaranteeing the governor airtime.[3] In Primorskii Krai, Shvydkoi appointed Valerii Bakshin to run the local broadcasting company, 'Vladivostok', in September 1998. The move was unsuccessfully opposed by Sergei Dudnik, the chairman of the regional Duma, on the grounds that Bakshin would serve the interests of his rival, regional governor Nazdratenko.[4]

In an effort to ensure their re-election, some regional leaders have persuaded the electoral commission in their region to disqualify serious rivals, and have promoted a nominal figure to comply with the legal requirement that at least two candidates must stand. Murtaza Rakhimov, the president of Bashkortostan, used these methods among others to ensure his re-election by an overwhelming majority on 14 June 1998. Although the Federal Supreme Court ruled against the result, it lacked political support, and its decision was evaded by the local electoral commission. The heads of 11 regions and republics appealed to Yeltsin to curtail the 'unfounded interference' of federal organs in the regional elections.[5] Stroev secured 93.6% of the vote in Orel Oblast against only nominal opposition in October 1996. Ilyumzhinov and Shaimiev dispensed with even nominal opponents in elections in 1995 and 1996 respectively.

Despite the propensity of regional leaders to bend election rules, six incumbents were defeated in the eight elections held in the first half of 1998. Notwithstanding their high political profile, few regional leaders are stronger than the vested economic and business interests that stand behind them, and business magnates can easily change, or divide, their loyalties. Alternative centres of power are emerging in the regions, chiefly in their principal cities. The municipalities and below count as local, rather than regional, government, and are not part of the 'system of state power' as defined by the constitution. This means that their officials are not directly subordinate to the next highest echelon, which is regional government. In August 1995, a 'Law on Local Self-Government' deprived the regional executive of the power to appoint local-government officials. Two years later, another law sought to give local authorities greater financial independence from 'their' regions. Although at most levels of local government, traditional subser-vience and a lack of resources have rendered the law ineffective, large municipalities have gained increasing influence. In most of Russia's regions, the principal town is the industrial base and main source of revenue. Yekaterinburg, for example, is a net contributor to the budget of Sverdlovsk Oblast, from which it recovers a proportion for its own expenditure. In Soviet times, the regional party boss retained the upper hand because he controlled the countryside that fed the town. Inertia has helped to maintain this hierarchy in post-Soviet Russia but, with large cities now able to shop around for their supplies, mayors are becoming increasingly serious rivals.

Constraints on Regional Power

The move to elected governors weakened, but did not break, the federal centre's power over the regions. Politically, the most significant instruments of central control are the Presidential Representatives: officials appointed by Yeltsin since 1991 to check that regional legislation does not contradict federal laws, and to coordinate federal agencies in the regions. Where necessary, these officials are also tasked with asserting the president's authority, but have been unable to do so against elected governors determined to resist them. In 1997, Yeltsin appointed Viktor Kondratov, the Federal Security Service (FSB) chief in Primorskii Krai, as his representative in the region, granting him exceptional powers to control its finances. The appointment was part of an attempt to bring down Nazdratenko, whom Yeltsin accused of corruption and abuse of power. Nazdratenko remained in office without changing his leadership style and, in February 1999, Kondratov was reassigned.

Federal offices, rather than Presidential Representatives, are in practice the most powerful instruments of direct central authority.

There are between 30 and 50 federal agencies in each region, including departments of the security bodies, the Ministry of Finance, the Central Bank, tax and customs agencies, and judicial organs. In April 1999, Primakov acknowledged that, excluding the Ministry of Internal Affairs and Tax Police, there were 330,000 central officials in the regions, more than in the Soviet era.[6]

In Russia's early post-independence years, there was little control over the circulation of money between the centre and the regions. Since 1995, however, the Federal Ministry of Finance has channelled financial flows to all ministries except defence through its own treasuries in the regions.

local courts are vulnerable to pressure from regional authorities

Although employees in the regions can be subject to local pressure, and some regions such as Sverdlovsk have ensured that they oversee appointments, central fiscal control has been maintained. The federal judiciary is less able to resist regional pressure. According to the constitution, federal law is paramount, and the financing and organisation of the courts are federal tasks. However, the central authorities often fail to meet their financing responsibilities, making local courts vulnerable to pressure from regional authorities reluctant to give up the long-standing Soviet tradition of 'telephone law', whereby the local judiciary operated at the behest of the local Communist Party boss. The creation of a new Judicial Department of the Supreme Court in 1998 is intended to protect the judiciary's independence, but informal influence is still commonplace, including in local Moscow courts. Complications also arise over the compatibility of federal and regional legislation. By mid-1999, the federal Ministry of Justice had identified some 50,000 regional legislative acts that did not comply with the constitution, or with federal laws. In many cases, discrepancies are the result of a regional legislature overtaking the sluggish federal law-making process. Saratov and Tatarstan, for example, have adopted liberal laws on the sale of agricultural land in the absence of any federal legislation in this area. In mid-1999, the Duma was preparing a much more restrictive Land Code.

The Constitutional Court, which adjudicates disputes between the centre and the regions, is potentially the most powerful federal legal instrument. The court has in some cases shown itself determined to uphold federal positions; in January 1997, for example, it ruled against Udmurtia's move to do away with elected local government.[7] However, the ruling succeeded thanks only to Yeltsin's active political support, and in general the court lacks teeth. An important finding in April 1996 against Moscow city and other regions which had unconstitutionally reintroduced the Soviet practice of *propiska* – restricting the right of free movement by forcing would-be residents to register – has been widely flouted.[8] The court faces three challenges that it must overcome if it is to establish its authority. First, it is operating in a context where observance of the law is seen by many regional and central figures as a matter of political expediency, rather than an obligation. Second, the court as currently constituted began its work only in 1995 following the suspension of its predecessor, which had become embroiled in the political battle between Yeltsin and the parliament (its chairman, Valerii Zorkin, was one of the president's leading opponents). As a result, it is wary of doing anything which could call its impartiality into question. The court tends to avoid confrontation by producing delphic judgements, its understanding of its brief is narrow and it seeks only to interpret the constitution, rather than actually making law. Finally, the power-sharing treaties between the centre and the regions have undermined the court's authority because some sanction extra-constitutional regional legislation. The 1994 treaty with Tatarstan, for example, grants the republic's constitution the same weight as that of the federation as a whole – but the Tatar constitution gives the republic international status, which the federal one prohibits. The June 1999 federal legislation covering these power-sharing treaties should make possible an agreed body of law governing relations between the centre and the regions, but this will take decades. In the meantime, the treaties are politically unassailable.

The Regions' Collective Influence

The regions' main vehicle for exerting pressure at the centre is the Federation Council, the upper house of parliament. The council enjoys considerable powers:

- all laws passed by the Duma (the lower house), including the annual budget, are subject to its approval;

- it controls senior legal appointments;
- it authorises the use of Russian armed forces abroad; and
- it has the final say in the impeachment of a president.

The Federation Council has exercised its powers where regional interests were directly affected. It blocked the 1999 budget until expenditure was tilted in favour of the regions, for example. The council has also blocked Yeltsin's senior judicial appointments. In 1994, it refused to approve his choice of procurator-general, Aleksei Ilyushenko, which meant that Ilyushenko had to serve his term in an acting capacity. Five years later, the council did not approve Yeltsin's dismissal of Ilyushenko's successor, Yurii Skuratov.

For all its constitutional powers, regional influence through the Federation Council has been limited. The council's weakness stems partly from its composition and voting procedures which, since they were the result of hasty compromise, are far from perfect. Council members are all fully occupied in their localities, and so cannot meet for more than two days each month. Although regional leaders travel to Moscow punctiliously for their sessions, they often spend their time lobbying in ministries rather than attending to legislative business in the council chamber. The council can barely cope with its legislative workload, and has had to resort to a form of postal voting. Regional leaders are often ill-informed about the issues, relying on guidance from their staff. There is also ill-feeling between the Federation Council and the Duma. The lower house is often frustrated at the way in which the council handles the laws that it drafts, while the council sometimes has to drop its own legislative initiatives after they have been rendered unrecognisable in the Duma. The Federation Council can block legislation passed by the Duma, though the lower house can overcome this veto by a two-thirds' majority. In September 1998, the Duma ignored the council's recommendation that Viktor Chernomyrdin be confirmed as prime minister.

The weakness of the Federation Council reflects the difficulty of accommodating the existing structures of government to the shift of gravity away from the centre to the regions. There is no breakdown of the Russian Federation into units broader than its 89 components. The Soviet division of Russia into 11 economic regions has been retained, but operates only as a source of statistical reporting and analysis. Since 1990, eight Inter-regional Economic Associations have been created, covering areas of the Urals, the Greater Volga, the North Caucasus, the Far East and Transbaikal zone, Siberia, the Black Earth zone, and north-west and central Russia. Membership is voluntary, and sometimes overlapping. These associations could be a good basis for consolidation. In the wake of the 1998 crisis, Primakov invited the chairmen of the associations to join the government's presidium, which comprises the prime minister and his deputies. The associations provide a useful means for the central government to address groups of regions. However, hints by Primakov in a policy-making speech in January 1999 that they might form the political core of a new federal structure met with a strongly negative response from the leaders of the republics, who saw any consolidation that brought them together with 'ordinary' regions as an infringement of their special status.[9] The associations maintain their coherence largely because their rotating chairmanships ensure that they have no political weight.

If the regions have little direct influence on the policies of the centre, their indirect impact through the electoral process is growing. This has had a largely negative effect, since the consolidation of power by regional élites has stunted the growth of national political parties in the regions. Under Russia's electoral law, half of the 450 Duma deputies are selected from a party

the regions' indirect impact through the electoral process is growing

list, and half directly elected in constituencies. A political party or movement must win at least 5% of the votes cast on its party list to be entitled to representation in the Duma as a parliamentary faction. Factions have a seat on the Council of the Duma, the lower house's controlling body, which allows them to influence how the Duma conducts business. In the Duma elected in December 1995, four parties crossed the 5% threshold:

- the Communist Party of the Russian Federation (CPRF) under Zyuganov;
- the NDR, set up in April 1995 as the 'party of power' under Chernomyrdin;
- Vladimir Zhirinovskii's nationalist Liberal Democratic Party of Russia (LDPR); and

- Grigorii Yavlinskii's liberal-cum-social democratic *Yabloko*.

None of these parties has since strengthened its position in the provinces. The CPRF is best placed to do so, having inherited much of the Soviet Communist Party's organisation. The LDPR and *Yabloko* both have regional structures, but the former is likely to fade along with its leader, while the latter has yet to develop the strength in numbers that would make it a decisive political force. The NDR did well in the provinces initially, since it attracted the regional élites and the administrative structures that they controlled, but lost its cohesion the moment Chernomyrdin was dismissed as prime minister in March 1998, confirming that it had never graduated from being the 'party of power' to becoming a real political organisation with a viable programme of its own. In the absence of strong national parties, provincial politicians with wider ambitions have found it difficult to find a national platform, and most are unknown outside their own region. Even when Nemtsov was the high-profile governor of Nizhnii Novgorod Oblast in 1991–97, with Yeltsin's more-or-less explicit backing as a future president, his national ratings were low.

In mid-1999, the regional élites were competing to take the NDR's place, and two broad electoral alliances, both of which involved regional and national politicians, had begun to emerge:

- Fatherland–All Russia, a left-of-centre alliance led by Luzhkov, Shaimiev and Vladimir Yakovlev, the mayor of St Petersburg. On 17 August, Primakov agreed to lead it into the Duma elections in December 1999; and
- the Union of Rightist Forces, including Samara Oblast Governor Konstantin Titov's Voice of Russia and the reformist political movement Just Cause, led by Nemtsov.

Both groups encompassed a wide range of political views, and neither was expected to survive beyond the presidential elections in July 2000. Nonetheless, the fact that they had been formed at all demonstrated the growing interdependence of regional and national politics. It was significant that a powerful regional politician such as Luzhkov sought the support of Primakov, a national political figure, and that Primakov should base his political comeback, following his dismissal as prime minister in May 1999, on a regional alliance.

Political relations between the regions and the centre have developed in a piecemeal fashion, through individual deals and amid rivalry between regions for attention and funding. The political power of regional leaders within their territories, and the influence of these territories over the federal authorities, is limited. The structure and institutions of the state make collective action by the regions rare and largely ineffective. Although regional and central political élites are becoming increasingly interdependent, conflicts with the centre remain endemic. These are, however, conducted with a view to gaining relative advantage, rather than independence from Russia. This is the background against which the strategic aspects of relations between the centre and the regions must be viewed.

chapter 4

The Strategic Dimension

The New Periphery

Russia's independence left many of its regions exposed as never before to the outside world. Under the Soviet Union, Russia had the trappings, but not the powers, of a sovereign state. Its Ministry of Foreign Affairs was a hollow institution, and most of its borders were no more than administrative boundaries with other Union Republics. International border regimes were the responsibility of the Union authorities. Overnight in December 1991, the administrative boundaries of 27 of Soviet Russia's regions became international frontiers of the Russian Federation (see Table 3, page 50). The country acquired the world's longest land border, at 14,509 kilometres; in all, 35 of its regions share a frontier with 14 foreign states. With republics and regions asserting their sovereignty, Russia's stability and territorial integrity were at risk from the start.

This threat was not, however, as grave as it may have first appeared. Neither of the two most separatist-minded republics, Tatarstan and Bashkortostan, has an international border, making secession difficult. The regions at Russia's periphery are overwhelmingly Russian in their ethnic make-up, and Moscow is their natural pole of attraction. The only exception is the North Caucasus, where Russians are a minority in each of the six republics bordering Georgia and Azerbaijan. Of these, only Chechnya has sought independence. Although Ukraine's claim to control the Russian side of the straits between the Azov and Black seas has not been settled, Russia has faced no major fresh claims to its territory from the newly

Table 3 *Russia's New Frontier Regions*

Region	'New' International Border
Republic of Altai	Kazakstan
Altai Krai	Kazakstan
Novosibirsk Oblast	Kazakstan
Omsk Oblast	Kazakstan
Tyumen Oblast	Kazakstan
Kurgan Oblast	Kazakstan
Chelyabinsk Oblast	Kazakstan
Orenburg Oblast	Kazakstan
Saratov Oblast	Kazakstan
Volgograd Oblast	Kazakstan
Astrakhan Oblast	Kazakstan
Republic of Dagestan	Azerbaijan, Georgia
Chechen Republic	Georgia
Republic of Ingushetia	Georgia
Republic of North Ossetia	Georgia
Kabardino-Balkar Republic	Georgia
Karachaevo-Cherkess Republic	Georgia
Krasnodar Krai	Georgia
Bryansk Oblast	Ukraine, Belarus
Rostov Oblast	Ukraine
Voronezh Oblast	Ukraine
Belgorod Oblast	Ukraine
Kursk Oblast	Ukraine
Smolensk Oblast	Belarus
Kaliningrad Oblast	Lithuania
Pskov Oblast	Belarus, Latvia, Estonia
Leningrad Oblast	Estonia

independent post-Soviet states. Estonia and Latvia dropped their claims to small areas in 1998, although Russia has delayed border agreements with both countries. Japan's claim to the southern Kurile Islands (Northern Territories) and a border dispute with China were inherited from the Soviet Union.

The CIS Borderlands

Only two of Russia's new frontier regions, Pskov and Leningrad bordering Latvia and Estonia, have acquired secure, demarcated international borders. (The border between Kaliningrad Oblast and Lithuania is not fully delimited.) The rest have 'soft' borders – with Azerbaijan, Belarus, Georgia, Kazakstan and Ukraine – where only the main crossing-points are controlled. Demarcating and controlling all of these frontiers would be expensive and virtually impossible and, after initial confusion, Moscow encouraged its new border regions to make their own arrangements with their neighbours.[1]

Russia's failure to control its borders has allowed smuggling and drug-trafficking to flourish; in June 1999, FSB Director Vladimir Putin – appointed prime minister in August – claimed that 80% of the drugs entering Russia crossed the Kazak border.[2] Russian Border Troops have been withdrawn from every member of the Commonwealth of Independent States (CIS) except Tajikistan and Belarus, and regional leaders on Russia's periphery appear to have been left to deal with the situation as best they can. In January 1999, Saratov Governor Ayatskov threatened to close the border between his region and Kazakhstan to halt the smuggling of drugs, arms and alcohol.[3]

Despite these problems, Moscow has assigned a special role to cross-border cooperation, particularly with the CIS countries. According to Eduard Kuzmin, a senior Russian Foreign Ministry official responsible for the ministry's ties with the regions, this cooperation 'responds to [Russia's] long-term interests as it ultimately leads *frontier relations remain* **ad hoc** *and unstable* to the creation of a "good-neighbourliness" belt' around Russia's perimeter.[4] Many Russians still regard Ukraine and Belarus as part of their homeland, and fostering good relations is a useful way of easing the pain inflicted by the loss of these republics in 1991. Good inter-regional relations also compensate for the often difficult relationship at state level between Russia and the other CIS countries.

In 1997, Russia signed a Treaty of Friendship recognising Ukraine's territorial integrity, thus ruling out any claims to Crimea, considered by many Russian politicians, notably Luzhkov, to be a part of Russia. The treaty also allowed for bilateral agreements between individual Russian and Ukrainian regions. One such agreement was signed between Voronezh Oblast and Luhansk Oblast in Ukraine in February 1999. For Russia, these agreements are valuable because they maintain the traditional ties with Ukraine which were threatened with the Soviet Union's collapse. Russia has not fulfilled its obligations under a separate protocol, signed at the same time as the Friendship Treaty, to delimit its border. This has fuelled suspicions in Kiev that Moscow has not given up its dream of winning the country back, and the situation in the border region remains unsettled. Customs arrangements with Ukraine are haphazard, and are regulated both by the federal and regional administrations, which are usually in dispute with each other.[5]

The 7,500km-long frontier with Kazakstan has also caused problems. Soviet-era economic links remain vital to Russia's border regions; Omsk Oblast, for example, depends on coal supplies from the neighbouring Kazak town of Ekibastuz. It cannot, however, pay for this fuel in cash because it operates a largely cashless economy. The local Kazak authorities will not accept barter as payment, and have threatened to cut off supplies.[6] Kazakstan also tried to close its border to cheap food imports from Russian regions following the 1998 financial crash. Uncontrolled emigration from Kazakstan to Russia, fuelled by Russia's higher living standards, is another potential problem. Perceived ethnic domination by Kazaks, and the consequent rise in the homeless and jobless populations in Russian border regions, has led to a revival of Cossack movements, the traditional guardians of Russia's southern borders.

Since 1997, Russia and Belarus have been actively seeking reunification. A union between the two countries is popular in Russia because it would partially restore the Slavic unity that was lost with the Soviet Union's collapse. For Belarus, it would provide an escape route from the country's economic difficulties. The impact of a union on Russia's delicately balanced constitutional settlement would, however, be profound. The form of the proposed union is vague: each country could retain its sovereignty, while sharing a presidency; Belarus could be absorbed into the Russian Federation as its ninetieth region; or its eight regions could be incorporated individually. The third option is likely to prove unacceptable to Belorussian President Alexander Lukashenka, while the first two would reopen the question of the status of Russia's existing components. Tatarstan has made clear that it will not accept a status beneath Belarus. This position appears to give Tatarstan an effective veto over any union since good relations with the republic are likely to be more important to the centre than accommodating Belorussian aspirations.

The North Caucasus

The republics of the North Caucasus present a distinct set of problems, largely because of Chechnya, the federation's only component not held in place by the constitutional settlement. Although Tatarstan, like Chechnya, refused to sign the Federation Treaty in 1992, there are crucial differences between the two republics. Tatar President Shaimiev is a seasoned Soviet-era leader, who donned nationalist clothing to increase his bargaining power with the centre, and to prevent more radical Tatar nationalists from outflanking him. Chechnya's Soviet-era leader, Doku Zavgaev, was overthrown by Air Force General Dzhokar Dudaev in 1991. Dudaev had been radicalised by the Estonian drive for independence, which he witnessed as commander of a Soviet strategic-bomber division in the Estonian town of Tartu in 1988–90. Even before he seized power, Chechnya's politics had been particularly fragmented, tribalised and criminalised by its geography and history. The mountainous republic had been abolished by Stalin in 1944 and its population deported, only to be reconstituted in 1957 within different boundaries.

Chechnya's bid for independence degenerated into civil strife. Moscow's clumsy and violent response, Dudaev's hysterical rhetoric and his inability to control organised crime and his radical followers led to war in 1994–96. The Chechen conflict penetrated deep into Russia's political, military and social life, not least because of the involvement of conscripts from regions all over Russia.[7] But Chechnya's particular circumstances meant that the war neither fuelled separatist sentiment in the rest of Russia, nor seriously

Map 2 *The North Caucasus*

destabilised the North Caucasus as a whole. All but one of the other North Caucasian republics – neighbouring Ingushetia – were still under the leadership of Soviet-era Communist Party bosses, whose main concern was that the conflict did not disturb ethnic relations in their territories. The most destabilising period for the North Caucasus has actually developed since the Chechen war ended. The peace agreement of 31 August 1996 provided for the complete withdrawal of federal armed forces from Chechnya, but postponed a decision on the republic's status until 2001. Chechnya is in limbo – constitutionally still a part of Russia, economically dependent on the federal authorities, politically outside their control, but not recognised as independent by any foreign state. Meanwhile, the unity between Chechen leaders forged during the war has broken down.

Despite high ethnic and political tensions and outright banditry in Chechnya and Dagestan, the Baku–Groznyy–Novorossiisk pipeline, which runs through these republics and constitutes the 'northern route' for oil exports from the Caspian Basin, resumed operating in 1997. At the working level, and where mutual benefit is perceived, the federal authorities have usually found a way of cooperating with Chechnya. But by mid-1999, operations were frequently being halted amid Russian accusations that the Chechens were siphoning off oil, and Chechen claims that Russia was not paying its transit fees.

The activities of Chechen warlords and criminal gangs have undermined neighbouring Dagestan's stability; powerful Chechen field commander Shamil Basaev, for example, is seeking to radicalise Chechnya and bring about an anti-Russian rebellion in Dagestan in a bid to create a separate Muslim republic outside Russia's control. On 7 August 1999, Basaev and his allies occupied several villages in the west of the republic, bordering Chechnya. The federal authorities responded by launching air attacks on rebel positions. Basaev's action was denounced by both Chechnya and Dagestan, and did not appear to have widespread local support. Nonetheless, the incursion could have knock-on effects, which would disturb Dagestan's delicately balanced political system. Political offices are distributed among the republic's many nationalities, including Chechens, who make up 4.5% of the population. The absence of law and order in Chechnya is also affecting the southern districts of Stavropol Krai, its Russian-dominated neighbour to the north, which has suffered power cuts (electricity lines straddle the border), cattle raids and other incursions. The *after Chechnya, Dagestan?* federal authorities face the dilemma of attempting to secure the frontier with Chechnya without conceding demands from Stavropol residents for an international border regime, which would weaken the argument that Chechnya is still a component of the Russian Federation. Moscow has signalled that, while it has retreated from Chechnya, it does not intend to lose control of the rest of the North Caucasus. The federal authorities attempted to improve the coordination of local security in May 1998 by creating a new combined security headquarters in Stavropol, and later by strengthening security around Chechnya's borders, but without noticeable improvement.

There has been ethnic strife to the west of Chechnya, between Ingushetia and North Ossetia. Ingushetia, the smallest and poorest of the new Russian republics, was created in June 1992 out of the Chechen–Ingush Autonomous Republic, following the Chechens' declaration of independence. North Ossetia is the only Christian and traditionally pro-Moscow republic in the North Caucasus. Ingushetia's main concern is to regain territory lost to North Ossetia in the reconstruction of the North Caucasian republics in 1957. A failed attempt to regain this territory by force in October 1992 led to bloody clashes – the only large-scale ethnic violence thus far in the Russian Federation – as a result of which Ingushetia absorbed Ingush refugees from North Ossetia. In mid-1999, periodic violence was continuing in the disputed area.

Finally, the deliberate mismatch of Turkic and Circassian nationalities under Stalin has led to ethnic tensions in two republics further west, Kabardino-Balkaria and Karachaevo-Cherkessia. In Karachaevo-Cherkessia, the republic's first popular presidential elections were put off for fear of upsetting its ethnic balance. When the polls were finally held, in May 1999, they were won by Vladimir Semenov, a representative of the dominant non-Russian ethnic group, the Karachay. In response to rising ethnic tensions, the federal authorities effectively nullified the result, appointing as acting president Valentin Vlasov, an ethnic Russian from outside the republic.

There is little prospect of political Islam reaching the Islamic heartland of Russia, principally Tatarstan and Bashkortostan. The North Caucasus has a different culture, came to Islam relatively late, has always followed a separate (*sufi*) teaching and is administered by a different Muftiat from that of European Russia. But the predominantly Muslim republics of the North Caucasus may adopt Muslim forms of legal practice (*Shari'a* law has been officially declared in Chechnya) that would alienate the already dwindling Russian population and undermine Russia's single judicial system. Moscow cannot control developments in Chechnya itself, but has acquiesced in Ingushetia's incorporation of some national peculiarities into its legal system. There is also an international legal dimension to this issue: the Russian Federation is trying to meet its obligations to the Council of Europe, including abolishing the death penalty. Capital punishment is both legal and practised in Chechnya.

Instability in the North Caucasus has impinged on Russia's relations with Georgia and Azerbaijan. While not averse to seeing Russia weakened, Tbilisi is concerned that Chechen crime could spread across the border, and therefore does not encourage the republic's bid for independence. The Chechens have built a road to the border in order to exploit their only connection with the outside world that circumvents Russia, but Georgia has stalled on work on its side of the frontier. There is also a link between Chechnya and Georgia's breakaway province of Abkhazia in the west of the country. Basaev, for example, fought on the side of the Abkhaz separatists in 1992–93. While Russia must take some of the blame for encouraging Abkhaz separatism in the early 1990s, the federal authorities have an interest in supporting territorial integrity throughout the region, including in Georgia, and an economic blockade remains in place on Russia's border with Abkhazia. Nonetheless,

Abkhazia was permitted to attend a Russian regional economic cooperation meeting in early 1999, drawing protests from Tbilisi.[8]

Georgia's other separatist province, South Ossetia, has ethnic ties to the neighbouring Russian republic of North Ossetia. Ethnic violence flared in 1991–92, resulting in the migration of Georgians from South Ossetia, of Ossetians from Georgia's internal regions and of South Ossetians to the North. South Ossetia became closely linked to the Russian Federation's economy, with transport and energy supplies coming from the North. By mid-1999, the political situation had calmed, thanks to the presence of predominantly Russian peacekeeping forces, an Organisation for Security and Cooperation in Europe (OSCE) mission and good relations between Georgian President Eduard Shevardnadze and his North Ossetian counterpart, Aleksandr Dzasokhov.

In terms of Russia's relations with Azerbaijan, the Chechen issue brought border problems to the fore. When the Soviet Union collapsed, Russia and Azerbaijan agreed to treat the short border between them as an administrative boundary only, to avoid dividing a local ethnic group, the Lezgin. However, Russia, convinced that the Dagestan–Azerbaijan border was a conduit for foreign mercenaries and weapons destined for Chechnya, declared the frontier's formal closure in December 1994, prompting protests from the now-divided Lezgin. Although the border regime was relaxed in April 1996, tensions on both sides have persisted.

The Russian Far East

The Russian Far East was a strategic outpost under both Russian imperial and Soviet regimes. Apart from fisheries, the region's main economic activity was mining, which supplied minerals and metals for the national economy. This was a poor springboard for the different but equally vital strategic role the Far East seemed destined to play at the end of the Cold War – spearheading Russia's entry into the burgeoning Asia-Pacific economy. In 1986, Gorbachev outlined a major plan under which the region was to lead Soviet economic resurgence.[9] Ten years later, Yeltsin signed a decree supporting a $73bn development scheme.[10] However, there has been no significant domestic or foreign investment, despite the area's energy resources, notably oil and gas reserves off Sakhalin. In 1997, foreign investment stood at $140 million, just 3.6% of the Russian total.[11]

Along with the rest of the country, the Far East has declined; industrial production, for example, fell by 54% between 1990 and 1995.[12] The rise in transport costs to reflect the real distance between the Russian Far East and European Russia has made energy significantly more expensive. Privatisation allowed the remnants of the local Soviet *nomenklatura* to take control, contributing to the criminalisation of the economy, which has in turn discouraged foreign business. Rivalries between and within the principal regions over the development of port facilities and the distribution of energy resources have prevented the formation of a coherent approach to the outside world.[13] There are long-running confrontations between Nazdratenko and the centre over alleged corruption and mismanagement of Primorskii Krai's resources, and between the governor and his local rivals. In May 1999, Yeltsin signed an agreement with South Korean President Kim Dae Jung reviving long-dormant plans for a special zone for Korean investment in the port area of Nakhodka in Primorskii Krai. The project is administered by Sergei Dudnik, Nazdratenko's principal rival. Nazdratenko was conspicuously absent from the agreement's signing ceremony.[14]

Map 3 *The Russian Far East*

Cross-border trade with China has also been disappointing. Until the crisis of August 1998, Russian consumers shunned poor-quality Chinese goods, while regional authorities in Khabarovsk and Primorskii Krais, concerned about the growing Chinese population in their territories, have created an increasingly hostile climate.[15] In the 1920s and 1930s, the area was ethnically mixed, but Stalin's expulsion of Koreans and Chinese in 1937 left it one of the most Slavic areas of Russia. The current population of the five regions directly bordering China, the overwhelming majority of which is Russian or Ukrainian, is less than 7m. By contrast, the three neighbouring Chinese regions, Heilongjiang, Jilin and Liaoning, are home to more than 90m people.[16] This has fostered a sense of vulnerability among the Russian inhabitants of the Far East, which politicians appealing to Russian nationalism have exploited. In June 1998, the speaker of the federal Duma, Gennadii Seleznev, described the illegal settlement of Chinese and Koreans in the Far East as creeping territorial expansion, and called on local administrations and legislatures to oppose it.[17] Refusing to countenance immigration from Asia will, however, be a major barrier to economic growth in the region even if investment picks up, since the necessary labour can only come from China and Korea. It will also perpetuate the ethnic divide between the Russian Far East and its neighbours, making the region's acceptance into the Asia-Pacific community more difficult.[18]

From the Soviet Union, Russia inherited a territorial dispute with Japan over the Kurile Islands (Northern Territories), which come under the jurisdiction of Sakhalin Oblast. Igor Farkhutdinov, the region's governor, has insisted that the Kuriles will never be ceded, a position supported by Russian Foreign Minister Igor Ivanov when he visited Sakhalin in February 1999. Nonetheless, Farkhutdinov understands the benefits of the Kuriles' joint economic exploitation with Japan, and negotiations have proceeded. In November 1998, Russia and Japan announced that they would form a subcommittee covering joint economic activities on the islands.[19] Unresolved border problems with China are another Soviet legacy, principally involving Khabarovsk and Primorskii Krais. Although the status of two islands in the Amur River is still under discussion, regional representatives are included in the demarcation commissions and this is no longer a major local political issue.

The North West
Like the Far East, the Russian North West was one of the Soviet Union's strategically sensitive zones, and was protected by a strict border regime. The end of the Cold War offered an opportunity to restore the North West's geographic, ethnic, cultural and infrastructure links with its neighbours. Political conditions are favourable, and the groundwork for inter-regional cooperation has been laid. Russian regions are involved in the main international regional organisations. The Republic of Karelia, Murmansk and

Map 4 *The North West*

Arkhangelsk are members of the Regional Council of the Barents Euro-Arctic Region, while Russian frontier regions take part in European Union (EU) INTERREG programmes designed to promote cross-border cooperation.

Although Finland ceded territory to the Soviet Union in 1940 and 1944, Helsinki has no territorial claims. In 1997, the Finnish government launched its 'Northern Dimension' initiative, which is designed to coordinate existing regional programmes. Although it was adopted by the EU in December 1998, the initiative is limited to a coordinating role, and has no funding of its own. The Russian government welcomed it, as did the regions involved, but there is a deep divide between the Western emphasis on technical assistance, and the Russian regions' desire for swift direct investment.

Kaliningrad Oblast on the Baltic coast is the only Russian region physically separated from the rest of the federation. Part of the former German territory of East Prussia, it was awarded to the Soviet Union at the end of the Second World War, its status to be finalised in a peace treaty that was never signed. The region was heavily militarised in Soviet times, and remains strategically vital to Russia. In 1996, unofficial Russian sources hinted that tactical nuclear weapons might be deployed in Kaliningrad in response to any enlargement of NATO.[20] The Alliance expanded nonetheless, and Poland's accession in March 1999 has given Kaliningrad Russia's second border with NATO after the frontier with Norway. Kaliningrad is also Russia's only naval base on the Baltic. In August 1994, it was made a special defence area, reporting directly to Moscow. Some 14,500 troops and 1,800 naval-infantry personnel are stationed in the region, along with over 800 tanks and 40 attack helicopters.[21] Force levels are, however, well within the limits set by the Conventional Armed Forces in Europe (CFE) Treaty, signed in

November 1990. Immediately following the Soviet Union's collapse, some 50,000 ground troops had been deployed in Kaliningrad.[22]

The importance to Russia of retaining Kaliningrad is unquestioned, and there are in fact no external claims to it. Germany showed a brief interest in resettling ethnic Germans from Russia in the region in 1989–92. Since then, Germany has kept a low political profile, but has been active commercially; in July 1999, German car-maker BMW opened an assembly line. Poland and Lithuania are prevented from pressing any territorial claims for fear of damaging their applications to join the EU. After the Second World War, Kaliningrad was settled with Russians, Belorussians and Ukrainians, who still make up 94% of its population, and there is no separatist agitation in the region itself.

Although politically quiescent, Kaliningrad's economic situation has been troubled, with industrial production declining to 31% of its level in 1990, against the Russian average of 48%.[23] Kaliningrad is heavily dependent on the outside world (it imports 90% of its foodstuffs and consumer goods), and was particularly vulnerable to the impact of the rouble's collapse in August 1998. The region also relies on Lithuania for energy and transport links: its road and rail routes to Russia cross Lithuania and Belarus, while Lithuania coordinates civilian air traffic to and from the region. The only link that remains as it was in Soviet days is the sea route to St Petersburg.

Kaliningrad's future is bound up with the enlargement of NATO and the EU. Since Poland and Lithuania need to meet EU requirements if their membership applications are to succeed, both countries have strengthened their border controls to keep out immigrants from non-EU countries. This poses a threat to Kaliningrad's economic viability, which depends on easy cross-border movement, including a visa-free regime with Lithuania. To compensate for its disadvantages, Kaliningrad was made a Free Economic Zone in early 1991, but this status was withdrawn by presidential decree in 1995. The following year, Kaliningrad was designated a Special Economic Zone (SEZ), which allows goods to be imported tax-free. Goods can also be exported to the rest of Russia free of tax provided that their value has been sufficiently increased, or they are assembled locally. The many loopholes in the SEZ legislation have, however, encouraged smuggling and other crime, while doubts about the zone's durability, together with

Map 5 *Kaliningrad*

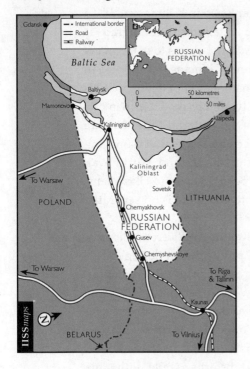

political uncertainty, have discouraged investment. The Russian authorities face several dilemmas over Kaliningrad's future. The region could be maintained as a strategic outpost, but this would be inimical to its development as an area of international economic activity. Russia could either seek a special status for Kaliningrad as an enclave within the EU, in order to extract maximum economic benefit from the region's position. Alternatively, it could emphasise Kaliningrad's equality with the federation's other components, in order to forestall any aspirations in the region itself for enhanced status, or any competing claims for special status from other strategically significant regions, such as Sakhalin. These difficult choices ensure that Kaliningrad will remain a sensitive issue in Russia's external and internal politics for many years to come.

The Regions and Russia's Foreign Relations

Under the constitution, the major elements of Russia's foreign and security policies are a federal responsibility. According to Article 71, they are:

- foreign policy, international relations and international treaties;
- questions of war and peace;
- foreign economic relations; and
- defence and security, including the production, sale and purchase of weapons.

Apart from Chechnya, no republic or region has challenged this federal prerogative, although Tatarstan has come close. A draft law allowing the republic's inhabitants to declare their citizenship as either Russian or Tatar on their passports would pose a serious challenge to the centre, both constitutionally (the Russian constitution allows for only single citizenship) and practically. The political understanding between Shaimiev and Yeltsin that underlay the bilateral treaty of 1994 has, however, prevented issues such as this from causing a serious rift. Only rarely have regions taken foreign-policy positions that differ from those of the federal authorities. Most disagreements arise over the centre's policies regarding the recognition of states. In mid-1998, representatives from seven republics – Bashkortostan, Dagestan, Sakha (Yakutia), Tatarstan, Tuva, Khakassia and Chuvashia – attended a conference in Istanbul which recognised the Turkish Republic of North Cyprus.[24] In 1999, Foreign Ministry official Kuzmin claimed that some regions had 'deviated' from Russia's 'fundamental policy principles in relations with Taiwan and in interacting with the UN'.[25]

Although a federal responsibility, Russian foreign policy must take account of regional interests in a way that Soviet foreign policy never did. The central government cannot reach agreements with neighbouring states without consulting the relevant regions, nor can it implement treaties governing the destruction of weapons of mass destruction (WMD) without regional cooperation. Regional opposition is complicating Russia's attempts to meet its obligations under the Chemical Weapons Convention (CWC), which it ratified in 1997. The six affected regions – Bryansk, Kirov, Kurgan, Penza, Saratov and Udmurtia – are demanding extra financing to compensate for the environmental damage that they claim would follow the destruction of chemical weapons. It has also proved difficult to find an acceptable site for a US-sponsored plant to burn off fuel from nuclear missiles due to be scrapped.[26] In framing its Balkan policies, the centre is constrained from adopting an overly pro-Slav stance for fear of antagonising Muslim-dominated Tatarstan and Bashkortostan. Finally, the federal government needs regional cooperation in attracting foreign investment, and in marketing exports, including arms.

Russian foreign policy must take account of regional interests

While foreign and security policy is assigned to the centre, coordinating the regions' international contacts and implementing the federation's international treaties are joint federal–regional responsibilities. In January 1999, Yeltsin signed the first law laying out the framework for the regions' foreign relations.[27] The legislation allows the regions to maintain relations below government level, and to sign agreements provided that these do not contradict federal legislation, impinge on other regions or purport to be international treaties. Regions may set up missions abroad (11 had done so by mid-1999), while equivalent regions of foreign states can establish missions in Russia, as long as these do not have a diplomatic function. Powerful and publicity conscious regional leaders, such as Shaimiev, Ayatskov and Rossel, have led large regional delegations abroad. But most regions have little experience of operating in an international environment and need the guidance of the federal authorities. In 1994, a department within the Ministry of Foreign Affairs was set up to handle contacts with the regions, while a 'Consultative Council of the Units of the Federation on International and Foreign Economic Contacts' meets every six months, and has drawn up model agreements between regions and their foreign partners. The Ministry of Foreign Affairs has some 25 offices in the provinces.

In terms of foreign economic relations, regional leaders are keen to attract investment, and negotiate with the federal authorities for tax concessions to help them in doing so. In general, foreign businesses do not prosper in a Russian region without the approval of the local authorities. These authorities frequently have an economic stake in local enterprises, and in any case set the tone for economic activity. But the governor's voice in the negotiation of a contract, especially with a large concern with headquarters in Moscow, is unlikely to be decisive. Raw materials and land are also highly charged political issues that cannot be dealt with solely at regional level.

Regions on the new periphery have capitalised on their 'gateway' position by setting up SEZs to encourage import–export operations. An Organisation for Economic Cooperation and Development (OECD) study in 1997 identified 24 such zones, but observed that most were believed not to function.[28] Political, rather than economic, considerations lie behind the centre's agreement to the creation of SEZs. The first ten zones were set up between July and September 1990, just after Soviet Russia declared its sovereignty. A further four were established by presidential decree in June 1996, just days before the presidential elections. Some SEZs were little more than money-making opportunities for regional élites and, in late 1998, the federal government decided to overhaul the system so that at least some of the profits accrued to the centre.

In January 1999, long-awaited amendments to a 1995 law on production-sharing agreements (PSAs) were introduced. Although enabling legislation is required before the law can come into effect, it should boost foreign investment in resource-rich regions because it allows prospectors in specified oil and gas fields to repatriate a share of the profits from their investment. It also grants them a favourable local tax regime. Participants in an approved scheme will, however, have to buy 70% of their equipment and hire 80% of their labour force in the Russian Federation.

Tensions between the centre and the regions have also surfaced concerning the country's crisis-hit defence industry. In the ten years from 1987, the value of Soviet/Russian arms exports fell from $31bn to $2.5bn; the country's share of the global market slumped from 35% to 5%.[29] This decline has particularly affected defence-dependent regions in the Greater Volga area, where arms production accounts for 30% of the local economy.[30] There is ambiguity over where control of the arms industry lies. According to the constitution, weapons production comes under federal juris-diction, but the power-sharing treaties between the centre and those regions with a significant arms industry have generally made the actual operation of defence enterprises a joint responsibility. Regional leaders are concerned to maintain the viability of their defence producers, and have opposed moves that could threaten their future. In 1997–98, for example, central-government plans to privatise a *Sukhoi* aircraft factory in Komsomolsk-na-Amure, Khabarovsk Krai, prompted strong protests from Governor Viktor Ishaev.[31] As a result, a fully government-owned corporation was set up, shares in which were allocated to the relevant regional administrations.[32]

Regional leaders are enjoying increasingly wide discretion in the overseas marketing of defence products. In May 1999, state arms-sales concern *Rosvooruzheniye* signed an agreement with Tatarstan which gave the republic greater freedom to sell abroad. In January 1999, Marii El President Vyacheslav Kislitsyn wrote to Kuwaiti Prime Minister Sheikh Saad al-Abdullah al-Salim al-Sabah offering to sell an S-300V air-defence system and other military equipment, components of which are manufactured in Kislitsyn's republic. While *Rosvooruzheniye* raised no objections to the proposed sale, the General Staff of the Russian armed forces declared that regional administrations were neither entitled to sell weapons, nor to approach potential buyers.[33]

The Regions and Russia's Military

Regional authorities have always been closely involved in the affairs of the armed forces stationed on their soil. In the Soviet Union, the regional party leader invariably sat on the local Military Council, and military leaders were members of the regional Communist Party committee. The armed forces, with their own state farms, have long been an integral part of a region's economy, while the housing registers kept by local authorities were a key element in the annual conscription process. Local authorities still work with the military to tackle draft-dodging.[34]

Since the collapse of the Soviet Union, the federal authorities have found it increasingly difficult to finance the armed forces. Between 1992 and 1997, estimated military expenditure fell from $146bn – 12% of gross domestic product (GDP) – to $64bn, or 6% of GDP.[35] Federal Interior Ministry troops and other paramilitary forces are separately funded, and have fared better. Under a military-reform programme which began in 1998, the country's eight military districts will be reduced to six military 'zones', whose boundaries will eventually be common to all defence and law-enforcement agencies. The aim is to devolve command and control, and to increase the local coordination of all branches of the security forces.

the increasing influence of regional leaders over local military units

However, lack of funds means that military reorganisation is likely to continue on an *ad hoc* basis, with units gradually losing their ties to the centre as they become increas-ingly entwined in the economic and political life of the region in which they are based. During the Chechen conflict, 'Committees of Soldiers' Mothers' were established in the regions to protest against the dispatch of their sons to the war zone, prompting the Chuvash authorities to declare a ban on 'their' conscripts being sent to dangerous areas. In Tatarstan and Bashkortostan, residents have been granted the right to do their military service exclusively within their own republic, the first step in creating an indigenous force.

Inadequate central funding has compelled regional leaders to take over once-closed military towns that can no longer pay their way, to deal with explosions in dilapidated weapon-storage facilities and to cope with the social needs of redundant military personnel. Tatarstan has created a government commission to tackle the social problems of service personnel and their families, as well as a special department in its Employment Committee.[36] Debt-ridden defence installations, particularly in the Far East, contribute significantly to local energy problems and cash-flow crises. Nazdratenko has repeatedly complained that this, rather than mismanagement, is at the root of Primorskii Krai's economic troubles.[37] In April 1999, the authorities in Sakhalin Oblast cut off power to all military and other centrally funded security units with the express aim of drawing Moscow's attention to the region's problems.[38] On a day-to-day level, the penury of the armed forces has made local commanders increasingly dependent on regional élites for pay, food and housing. In return, they supply cheap labour to help with the harvest, or construct buildings for use by the regional authorities. Karelian Prime Minister Sergei Katanandov announced in September 1998 that, given the difficulties in provisioning the border troops in his republic, he had given them free licences to hunt elk.[39]

Regional leaders are increasingly using their patronage of the armed forces to gain publicity or political advantage. In August 1998, Samara Governor Titov was reportedly exploring the possibility of sponsoring a Pacific Fleet submarine, suggesting that it should be renamed 'Samara'.[40] Luzhkov sponsors the Black Sea Fleet based in Sevastopol, Ukraine, which he champions as a Russian city. In July 1998, shortly after being elected governor of Krasnoyarsk Krai, Lebed wrote an open letter to then Prime Minister Kiriyenko, suggesting that his region should be granted the status of a nuclear territory in exchange for feeding and paying the troops of the strategic-missile unit based in his territory. Shortly after NATO's bombing campaign against Yugoslavia began in March 1999, Ayatskov told his local legislature that *Topol*-M nuclear missiles and Tu-160 strategic bombers were based in Saratov in order to 'hit the aggressor in the teeth'.[41]

Despite the increasing influence of regional leaders over the military units stationed on their soil, alliances between local commanders and politicians, either to threaten the centre or to mount a local coup, are unlikely.[42] Russia has no tradition of military involvement in politics and, when the armed forces have been forced to assume a political role, as they were in 1991 and 1993, they have derived no benefits from doing so. While troops might support efforts by their commanders to improve their material conditions, they are unlikely to back attempts to achieve more distant political objectives. Neither the current military districts, nor the military zones planned under the reform programme, coincide with regional administrative boundaries. To forge an effective alliance with the commander of a military district, regional leaders would need to set aside their rivalries and coordinate their actions. They have shown no inclination or ability to do so. Even in Russia's poorest regions, members of the political élite are unlikely to jeopardise their privileges by militarily challenging the centre. In Volgograd in April 1998, the local political authorities actively frustrated attempts by General Lev Rokhlin to foment a military protest.

Despite the many challenges that it faces, Russia has remained relatively stable since the Soviet Union's collapse in 1991. The armed forces want decent living standards, not political power, while regional leaders are gaining a greater stake in national politics, and are unlikely to put their enhanced positions at risk by defying the centre militarily. Regional separatism does not pose a major threat to Russia's integrity, and there are no unmanageable external territorial claims. Accommodating Russia's new border regions to post-Cold War conditions will not be easy, but the process presents opportunities for fruitful contact, as well as raising risks of fragmentation.

The rise of regional power in post-Soviet Russia is a break with the country's centralised past almost as dramatic as the collapse of communism. It does not, however, mean that the country faces disintegration. Russia is the natural home of the overwhelming majority of its inhabitants; despite developments in Dagestan in August 1999, Chechen separatism is the exception, rather than the rule, and confrontations between the centre and the regions have almost exclusively been resolved through negotiation rather than violence. Although the regions have assumed a sometimes alarming degree of power, most remain economically and politically dependent on the centre. The most important regional leaders are developing a taste for national political power, while the heads of national parties are aware of the influence regional politicians exert on voting patterns in their territories. A deeper understanding of the interdependence of the centre and the regions seems to be emerging.

Whereas Yeltsin opted, at least in principle, for radical reform of Russia's political and economic systems, he drew back from changing the Soviet system of republics and regions, establishing instead a fluctuating and negotiable balance of power. Although a more rigorous attempt to rationalise the flawed federal structure would have placed the new Russian state under intolerable strain, stability in the short term has come at the expense of the country's long-term political and economic development. In the absence of an agreed framework of rules and regulations, privatisation became hostage to the interests of central and regional élites, which colluded to carve up former state assets between themselves. This has frustrated the grass-roots economic reform without which no workable national economic programme is possible. The freedom enjoyed by regional leaders to run their territories as they wish has stunted the growth of democracy in the regions, and has inhibited the development of national political parties. Although national–regional electoral alliances may be emerging, politics remains highly personalised, and the development of a national, party-based system will in any case always be difficult given Russia's size and diversity. Finally, the close relationship between regional authorities and local military units is conducive to the long-term integrity of neither the armed forces, nor the Russian state. In the short term, informal alliances between political and military units will not be used to exert direct political pressure on the centre. Both regional political leaders and local commanders are more interested in extracting funds from the centre than in challenging it militarily, while the rivalry between regional élites means that any attempt at coordinated action would in any case probably fail. Nonetheless, plans for greater autonomy and the regional consolidation of security structures need to be backed by sufficient funds to ensure that these informal alliances do not become destabilising.

Russia needs some form of federal structure, but this devolution of power must take place within a transparent legal framework. The current system, with

Russia needs some form of federal structure

its bilateral deals between the centre and the regions, is at best inefficient, at worst the prelude to uncontrolled decentralisation. However, given Yeltsin's weakened condition, any substantial changes to the current arrangement will only be possible after presidential elections in July 2000.

In the short term, the new president will need to support the reform of fiscal relations. This will necessitate new federal legislation covering the budget and taxation, overriding bilateral deals that favour one region over another. Establishing a regulated and transparent economy at regional level would go far towards removing the root causes of corruption, thereby forming the basis for the democratisation of regional politics. The new president will also need to ensure that the judiciary is adequately supported at all levels. This would allow courts to function independently of the regional authorities, making it easier to control errant governors. The Supreme Court and the Constitutional Court must be politically supported by the central authorities, even when their judgements are unwelcome.

In the longer term, the new president will need to begin a formal dialogue on the federation's future. This would not only serve notice of the centre's determination to adopt a hitherto absent regional policy, but also reassure regional politicians that they have a role to play in its formulation. This dialogue should attempt to mould into a new constitutional settlement the practices that have developed since Russia's independence. But to attract regional politicians, it would also need to examine interim solutions that do not necessitate constitutional change. These could include increasing formal regional influence at the centre by basing one of the two regional representatives in the Federation Council permanently in Moscow.

There are no external threats to Russia's integrity, and external factors are not crucial to the reform of the country's federal structure. Instability in Russia's CIS neighbours, notably Kazakstan and Ukraine, could upset the relationship between the centre and the regions, as would any form of union with Belarus. Nonetheless, on balance links at regional level between Russia and its CIS neighbours are a force for stability. While Chechnya's *de facto* separation appears unlikely to be reversed, the threat it poses to the stability of Russia as a whole is minimal. However, any attempt by states to the south to exploit Russia's weakness in the North Caucasus would make it more difficult to contain the problem. In the economically depressed Far East, both central and regional authorities need to take steps to create a favourable environment for foreign business, principally by establishing political stability in Primorskii Krai and overcoming regional resistance to foreign labour. Increased trade across the Russia–China border, Korean and Japanese investment and the exploitation of gas deposits off Sakhalin would all help to revive the region. Given its favourable political environment and traditional links with its neighbours, the North West could become a model of outside engagement with Russia's peripheral regions.[1] If the EU expands to include Poland and Lithuania, special arrangements will need to be made concerning Kaliningrad. For example, free movement in and out of the region will need to be balanced with the requirement to protect the EU's external borders.

The Russian state is in the process of reconstituting itself in the wake of the country's loss of empire. In the decade since Russia's independence, the centre's authority has declined, and it is unlikely that even an authoritarian leader could reconstruct a viable centralised state. As its regions regain their individual, diverse personalities, a 'Russia of the regions' may begin to take shape. A state built on the local units with which Russians themselves identify would be more difficult to govern than one based on some central edict. However, by taking regional diversity into account, such a state would be more stable and secure.

Russia's Administrative Units

Name Principal City	■ Area (km²) ▲ Population
	(Jan 1997)
Leader (term expires)	● Treaty with Centre
Ethnic mix (1989 census) *Characteristics*	

European North

Arkhangelsk Oblast Arkhangelsk
Head of Administration Anatolii Yefremov (2000)
93% Russian *Naval base; forestry*

■ 410,700 ▲ 1,472,700
● None

Republic of Karelia Petrozavodsk
Chairman of Government Sergei Katanandov (2002)
74% Russian 10% Karelian 7% Belorussian *Forestry; borders Finland*

■ 172,400 ▲ 780,100
● None

Republic of Komi Syktyvkar
Head of Republic Yurii Spiridonov (2001)
58% Russian 23% Komi 8% Ukrainian *Forestry, oil, coal, based on convict labour*

■ 415,900 ▲ 1,172,700
● 20 March 1996

Murmansk Oblast Murmansk
Head of Administration Yurii Yevdokimov (2000)
83% Russian 9% Ukrainian *Northernmost ice-free port*

■ 144,900 ▲ 1,030,100
● 30 October 1997

Note   Administrative units are listed by economic region

Sources   *Rossiiskie Regiony posle Vyborov – 96* (Moscow: Yuridicheskaya
Literatura, 1997); and Michael McFaul and Nikolai Petrov (eds),
Politicheskii Almanakh Rossii 1997 (Moscow: Carnegie Center, 1998)

Nenets Autonomous Okrug Naryan-Mar ■ 176,700 ▲ 48,100
Head of Administration Vladimir Butov (2000) ● None
66% Russian 11% Nenets 10% Komi 7% Ukrainian *Formally subordinate to Arkhangelsk Oblast*

Vologda Oblast Vologda ■ 145,700 ▲ 1,344,100
Governor Vyacheslav Pozgalev (2000) ● 4 July 1997
97% Russian *Nucleus of the Russian North*

North West

Kaliningrad Oblast Kaliningrad ■ 15,100 ▲ 935,100
Head of Administration (Governor) Leonid Gorbenko (2000) ● 12 January 1996
79% Russian 9% Belorussian 7% Ukrainian *Russia's only ice-free port on Baltic; HQ of Baltic Fleet; separated from Russia by Lithuania*

Leningrad Oblast St Petersburg ■ 85,900 ▲ 1,677,200
Vacant (elections 19 September 1999) ● 13 June 1996
91% Russian *Borders Finland and Estonia*

Novgorod Oblast Velikii Novgorod ■ 55,300 ▲ 738,500
Head of Administration Mikhail Prusak (1999) ● None
95% Russian *Historic past as city-state; light industry*

St Petersburg ■ 600 ▲ 4,838,000
Governor, Chairman of Government Vladimir Yakovlev (2000) ● 13 June 1996
89% Russian *Capital, 1712–1918; gateway to Baltic; defence industry*

Pskov Oblast Pskov ■ 55,300 ▲ 827,000
Head of Administration Yevgenii Mikhailov (2000) ● None
94% Russian *Borders Belarus, Estonia and Latvia*

Central

Bryansk Oblast Bryansk ■ 34,900 ▲ 1,473,000
Head of Administration Yurii Lodkin (2000) ● 4 July 1997
96% Russian *Wartime partisan centre; borders Ukraine and Belarus*

Ivanovo Oblast Ivanovo ■ 21,800 ▲ 1,255,500
Head of Administration Vladislav Tikhomirov (2000) ● 20 May 1998
96% Russian *Depressed textile region*

Kaluga Oblast Kaluga ■ 29,900 ▲ 1,095,900
Governor Valerii Sudarenkov (2000) ● None
94% Russian *Artists' dacha country; science centres*

Kostroma Oblast Kostroma ■ 60,100 ▲ 805,700
Head of Administration Viktor Shershunov (2000) ● 20 May 1998
96% Russian *Outskirts of central industrial region*

Moscow city ■ 1,200 ▲ 8,637,000
Mayor, Government Premier Yurii Luzhkov (2000) ● 16 June 1998
90% Russian *Capital, region and municipality*

Moscow Oblast Moscow ■ 47,000 ▲ 6,573,000
Head of Administration Anatolii Tyazhlov (1999) ● None
94% Russian *High-technology industry*

Orel Oblast Orel ■ 24,700 ▲ 914,000
Head of Administration Yegor Stroev (2001) ● None
97% Russian *'Black-earth' agricultural region*

Ryazan Oblast Ryazan ■ 39,600 ▲ 1,316,500
Head of Administration Vyacheslav Lyubimov (2000) ● None
96% Russian *Food industry*

Smolensk Oblast Smolensk ■ 49,800 ▲ 1,166,200
Head of Administration Aleksandr Prokhorov (2002) ● None
94% Russian *Main route between Moscow and the West*

Tula Oblast Tula ■ 25,700 ▲ 180,100
Governor Vasilii Starodubtsev (2001) ● None
95% Russian *Historic centre for manufacture of guns and samovars*

Tver Oblast Tver (formerly Kalinin) ■ 84,100 ▲ 1,652,900
Governor Vladimir Platov (1999) ● 13 June 1996
94% Russian *Erstwhile rival to Moscow as capital; economically depressed*

Vladimir Oblast Vladimir ■ 29,000 ▲ 1,636,900
Head of Administration Nikolai Vinogradov (2000) ● None
96% Russian *Centre of Russian state between twelfth and fifteenth centuries*

Yaroslavl Oblast Yaroslavl ■ 36,400 ▲ 1,443,000
Governor Anatolii Lisitsyn (1999) ● 20 October 1997
96% Russian *Industrial; cradle of political reform*

Volga Vyatka

Chuvash Republic Cheboksary ■ 18,300 ▲ 1,359,000
President Nikolai Fedorov (2001) ● 27 May 1996
68% Chuvash 27% Russian *Turkic; one of few titular majorities*

Kirov Oblast Kirov ■ 120,800 ▲ 1,622,900
Governor Vladimir Sergeenkov (2000) ● None
90% Russian *Politically quiescent*

Republic of Marii El Yoshkar Ola ■ 23,200 ▲ 764,300
President Vyacheslav Kislitsyn (2001) ● 20 May 1998
48% Russian 43% Mari 6% Tatar *Finno-Ugrian people*

Republic of Mordovia Saransk   ■ 26,200 ▲ 950,000
Head of Republic Nikolai Merkushkin (1999)   ● None
61% Russian 33% Mordva 5% Tatar *Finno-Ugrian people*

Nizhnii Novgorod Oblast Nizhnii Novgorod   ■ 76,900 ▲ 3,707,900
Governor Ivan Sklyarov (2001)   ● 8 June 1996
95% Russian *Formerly closed region of Gorky, now one of Russia's most open regions*

Central Black Earth

Belgorod Oblast Belgorod   ■ 27,100 ▲ 1,477,500
Head of Administration Yevgenii Savchenko (2003)   ● None
93% Russian 6% Ukrainian *Relatively prosperous; iron ore and agriculture*

Kursk Oblast Kursk   ■ 29,800 ▲ 1,341,300
Head of Administration Aleksandr Rutskoi (2000)   ● None
97% Russian *Rutskoi is Yeltsin's former vice-president*

Lipetsk Oblast Lipetsk   ■ 24,100 ▲ 1,247,700
Head of Administration Oleg Korolev (2002)   ● None
97% Russian *'Donor' region thanks to metals exports*

Tambov Oblast Tambov   ■ 34,300 ▲ 1,310,600
Head of Administration Aleksandr Ryabov (1999)   ● None
97% Russian *Edge of 'black-earth' zone; far from industrial centres*

Voronezh Oblast Voronezh   ■ 52,400 ▲ 2,495,400
Head of Administration Ivan Shabanov (2000)   ● 20 May 1998
93% Russian 5% Ukrainian *Potentially rich agricultural region*

Volga

Astrakhan Oblast Astrakhan   ■ 44,100 ▲ 1,029,300
Head of Administration Anatolii Guzhvin (2000)   ● 30 October 1997
72% Russian 13% Kazak 7% Tatar *Where Volga flows into Caspian Sea*

Republic of Kalmykia Elista   ■ 75,900 ▲ 318,500
President Kirsan Ilyumzhinov (2002)   ● None
45% Kalmyk 38% Russian *Buddhist outpost*

Penza Oblast Penza   ■ 43,200 ▲ 1,554,700
Head of Administration Vasilii Bochkarev (2002)   ● None
86% Russian 6% Mordva 5% Tatar *Agricultural; industrial backwater*

Samara Oblast Samara (formerly Kuibyshev)   ■ 53,600 ▲ 3,308,500
Governor Konstantin Titov (2000)   ● 1 August 1997
83% Russian 4% Chuvash 4% Mordva 4% Tatar *Leading reformist region; 'donor'; home to Moscow's industry during Second World War*

Saratov Oblast Saratov ■ 100,200 ▲ 2,725,800
Governor Dmitri Ayatskov (2000) ● 4 July 1997
86% Russian *Rivals Samara as 'capital of the Volga'*

Republic of Tatarstan Kazan ■ 68,000 ▲ 3,763,200
President Mintimer Shaimiev (2001) ● 15 February 1994
49% Tatar 43% Russian *Leading republic on Europe–Asia divide*

Ulyanovsk Oblast Ulyanovsk (formerly Simbirsk) ■ 37,300 ▲ 1,490,000
Head of Administration Yurii Goryachev (2000) ● 30 October 1997
73% Russian 12% Tatar 8% Chuvash 4% Mordva *Lenin's birthplace (Ulyanov)*

Volgograd Oblast Volgograd (formerly Stalingrad) ■ 113,900 ▲ 2,701,600
Head of Administration Nikolai Maksyuta (2000) ● None
89% Russian *Strategic region at Volga–Don confluence*

North Caucasus

Republic of Adygeya Maikop ■ 7,600 ▲ 450,500
President Aslan Dzharimov (2001) ● None
68% Russian 22% Adygei *Enclave within Krasnodar Krai*

Chechen Republic (Ichkeria) Dzhokar (Groznyy) ■ 15,000 ▲ 862,000
President and Government Chairman Aslan Maskhadov (2002) ● 12 May 1997
66% Chechen 25% Russian *Break-away republic; riven with internal feuding*

Republic of Dagestan Makhachkala ■ 50,300 ▲ 2,097,500
Chairman of State Council Magomedali Magomedov (2002) ● None
28% Avar 16% Dargin 16% Kumyk 11% Lezgin 9% Russian *Unique in having no titular nationality, no direct elections for leader*

Republic of Ingushetia Magas (Nazran until Oct 1998) ■ 4,300 ▲ 303,500
President Ruslan Aushev (1999) ● None
75% Ingush 13% Russian 10% Chechen *Smallest republic, until 1992 part of Chechen–Ingush Autonomous Republic*

Kabardino-Balkar Republic Nalchik ■ 12,500 ▲ 789,500
President Valerii Kokov (2001) ● 1 July 1994
48% Kabardinian 32% Russian 9% Balkar *Artificially unites Circassian Kabardinians, Turkic Balkars*

Karachaevo-Cherkess Republic Cherkessk ■ 14,100 ▲ 436,100
Acting President Valentin Vlasov ● None
42% Russian 31% Karachay 10% Cherkess 7% Abazin *Unstable mix of Turkic and Circassian ethnic groups*

Krasnodar Krai Krasnodar ■ 76,000 ▲ 5,039,000
Head of Administration Nikolai Kondratenko (2000) ● 30 January 1996
85% Russian *Bread-basket; deeply conservative*

Republic of North Ossetia-Alania Vladikavkaz ■ 8,000 ▲ 664,200
President Aleksandr Dzasokhov (2002) ● 23 March 1995
53% Ossetian 30% Russian *Pro-Moscow; only Christian republic in North Caucasus*

Rostov Oblast Rostov-on-Don ■ 100,800 ▲ 4,425,400
Head of Administration Vladimir Chub (2001) ● 11 June 1996
90% Russian *Most progressive Russian region in North Caucasus*

Stavropol Krai Stavropol ■ 66,500 ▲ 2,671,100
Governor, Government Chairman Aleksandr Chernogorov (2000) ● None
84% Russian *Agricultural; conservative*

Urals

Republic of Bashkortostan Ufa ■ 143,600 ▲ 4,080,200
President Murtaza Rakhimov (2002) ● 3 August 1994
39% Russian 28% Tatar 22% Bashkir *'Donor'; autocratically ruled by minority Bashkirs*

Chelyabinsk Oblast Chelyabinsk ■ 87,900 ▲ 3,675,400
Governor Petr Sumin (2000) ● 4 July 1997
81% Russian 6% Tatar *'Rust-belt' industry predominates*

Komi-Permyak Autonomous Okrug Kudymkar ■ 32,900 ▲ 158,800
Head of Administration Nikolai Poluyanov (2000) ● 31 May 1996 (within
61% Komi-Permyak 35% Russian Perm treaty)
Titular people form majority

Kurgan Oblast Kurgan ■ 71,000 ▲ 1,112,200
Head of Administration Oleg Bogomolov (2000) ● None
91% Russian *Politically quiescent agricultural appendage to Urals*

Orenburg Oblast Orenburg ■ 124,000 ▲ 2,228,600
Head of Administration Vladimir Yelagin (1999) ● 30 January 1996
72% Russian 7% Tatar 5% Kazak *Former colonial outpost, frontier district once again*

Perm Oblast Perm ■ 127,700 ▲ 2,852,300
Governor Gennadii Igumnov (2000) ● 31 May 1996
86% Russian 5% Tatar *Highly industrialised 'donor'*

Sverdlovsk Oblast Yekaterinburg ■ 194,800 ▲ 4,667,800
Head of Administration Eduard Rossel (1999) ● 12 January 1996
89% Russian *Yeltsin's home; 'donor'*

Udmurt Republic Izhevsk ■ 42,100 ▲ 1,640,700
Chairman of State Council Aleksandr Volkov ● 17 October 1995
59% Russian 31% Udmurt 7% Tatar *Militarised economy, parliamentary political system*

West Siberia

Republic of Altai Gorno-Altaisk   ■ 92,600 ▲ 202,100
Chairman of Government Semen Zubakin (2001)   ● None
60% Russian 31% Altai 6% Kazak *Thinly populated mountainous republic – 'Russian Tibet'*

Altai Krai Barnaul   ■ 169,100 ▲ 2,690,100
Head of Administration Aleksandr Surikov (2000)   ● 29 November 1996
90% Russian 5% German *Bread-basket of Siberia*

Khanty-Mansi Autonomous Okrug Khanty-Mansiisk ■ 523,100 ▲ 1,330,600
Governor Aleksandr Filipenko (2000)   ● None
66% Russian 12% Ukrainian 8% Tatar *Produces half of Russia's oil; titular peoples form just 2% of population; administratively subordinate to Tyumen Oblast*

Kemerovo Oblast Kemerovo   ■ 95,500 ▲ 3,042,200
Head of Administration Aman Tuleev (2001)   ● None
91% Russian *'Kuzbass' coal, metals heartland*

Novosibirsk Oblast Novosibirsk   ■ 178,200 ▲ 2,744,600
Head of Administration Vitalii Mukha (1999)   ● None
92% Russian *Defence industry; scientific centre*

Omsk Oblast Omsk   ■ 139,700 ▲ 2,174,200
Governor Leonid Polezhaev (1999)   ● 19 May 1996
80% Russian 6% German 5% Ukrainian *Oil refineries, defence industry*

Tomsk Oblast Tomsk   ■ 316,900 ▲ 1,071,800
Governor Viktor Kress (1999)   ● None
88% Russian *Politically quiescent*

Tyumen Oblast Tyumen   ■ 161,800 ▲ 1,351,100
Governor Leonid Roketsky (2001)   ● None
84% Russian 7% Tatar *Wealth derives from its autonomous* okrugs

Yamal-Nenets Autonomous Okrug Salekhard   ■ 750,300 ▲ 488,400
Governor Yurii Neyelov (2000)   ● None
59% Russian 17% Ukrainian 5% Tatar 4% Nenets *Produces 90% of Russia's gas; administratively subordinate to Tyumen Oblast*

East Siberia

Aga-Buryat Autonomous Okrug Aginsk settlement   ■ 19,000 ▲ 79,400
Head of Administration Bair Zhamsuev (2001)   ● None
54% Buryat 42% Russian *Enclave of Chita Oblast*

Republic of Buryatia Ulan Ude   ■ 351,300 ▲ 1,049,700
President Leonid Potapov (2002)   ● 29 August 1995
70% Russian 24% Buryat *Centre of Russian Buddhism*

Chita Oblast Chita ■ 412,500 ▲ 1,216,000
Head of Administration Ravil Geniatulin (2000) ● None
91% Russian *Overland gateway to China*

Evenk Autonomous Okrug Tura ■ 767,600 ▲ 20,300
Head of Administration Aleksandr Bokovikov (2001) ● 1 November 1997 (within
68% Russian 14% Evenk 5% Ukrainian Krasnoyarsk treaty)
Taiga; landing-place of Tunguz meteorite in 1911

Irkutsk Oblast Irkutsk ■ 745,500 ▲ 2,652,400
Governor Boris Govorin (2001) ● 27 May 1996
90% Russian *Largest* oblast, *rich in hydroelectricity*

Republic of Khakassia Abakan ■ 61,900 ▲ 584,100
Chairman of Government Aleksei Lebed (brother of Aleksandr) (2000) ● None
80% Russian 11% Khakas *Aluminium-rich; formerly part of Krasnoyarsk Krai*

Krasnoyarsk Krai Krasnoyarsk ■ 710,000 ▲ 3,038,200
Governor Aleksandr Lebed (2002) ● 1 November 1997
88% Russian *Federation's second-largest component*

Taimyr (Dolgano-Nenets) Autonomous Okrug Dudinka ■ 862,100 ▲ 46,500
Head of Administration Gennadii Nedelin (2000) ● 1 November 1997 (within
67% Russian 9% Dolgan 9% Ukrainian *Home of the* Krasnoyarsk treaty)
world's largest nickel concern, Norilsk Nikel

Republic of Tuva (Tyva) Kyzyl ■ 170,500 ▲ 309,700
President, Chairman of Government Sheringool Oorzhak (2001) ● None
64% Tuvan 32% Russian *Formally independent until 1944, still claims right to secede*

Ust-Orda Buryat Autonomous Okrug Ust-Orda settlement ■ 22,400 ▲ 142,800
Head of Administration Valerii Maleev (2000) ● 27 May 1996 (within
57% Russian 36% Buryat *Enclave of Irkutsk Oblast,* Irkutsk treaty)
agrarian stronghold

·Far East

Amur Oblast Blagoveshchensk ■ 363,700 ▲ 1,031,700
Head of Administration Anatolii Belonogov (2001) ● 20 May 1998
87% Russian 7% Ukrainian *Granary of Far East; defence industry*

Chukotka Autonomous Okrug Anadyr ■ 737,700 ▲ 99,700
Head of Administration Aleksandr Nazarov (2000) ● None
66% Russian 17% Ukrainian 7% Chukchi *Isolated, easternmost region, officially separated
from parent Magadan Oblast in 1992*

Jewish Autonomous Oblast Birobidzhan ■ 36,000 ▲ 206,700
Head of Administration Nikolai Volkov (2000) ● None
83% Russian 7% Ukrainian 4% Jewish *Failed Stalinist experiment to create Jewish
homeland*

Kamchatka Oblast Petropavlovsk-Kamchatsky   ■ 170,800 ▲ 411,100
Governor Vladimir Biryukov (2000)   ● None
81% Russian 9% Ukrainian *Isolated, volcanic; endemic fuel shortages*

Khabarovsk Krai Khabarovsk   ■ 788,600 ▲ 1,555,500
Head of Administration Viktor Ishaev (2000)   ● 24 April 1996
86% Russian 6% Ukrainian *Defence plants in industrialised south*

Koryak Autonomous Okrug Palana settlement   ■ 301,500 ▲ 32,800
Governor Valentina Bronevich (2000)   ● None
62% Russian 17% Koryak 7% Ukrainian *Subordinated to Kamchatka; only region with a female governor*

Magadan Oblast Magadan   ■ 461,400 ▲ 251,100
Governor Valentin Tsvetkov (2000)   ● 4 July 1997
72% Russian 16% Ukrainian *Gold mines, forced-labour camps*

Primorskii (Maritime) Krai Vladivostok   ■ 165,900 ▲ 2,238,800
Governor Yevgenii Nazdratenko (1999)   ● None
87% Russian 8% Ukrainian *Gateway to Japan, with the Far East's two major ports*

Republic of Sakha (Yakutia) Yakutsk   ■ 3,103,200 ▲ 1,022,800
President Mikhail Nikolaev (2000)   ● 29 June 1995
50% Russian 33% Yakut 7% Ukrainian *Federation's largest component; monopoly producer of diamonds*

Sakhalin Oblast Yuzhno-Sakhalinsk   ■ 87,100 ▲ 631,800
Governor Igor Farkhutdinov (2000)   ● 29 May 1996
82% Russian 7% Ukrainian 5% Korean *Comprises Sakhalin Island and Kurile chain*

Chapter 1

[1] See Ronald Grigor Suny, *The Revenge of the Past: Nationalism, Revolution and the Collapse of the Soviet Union* (Stanford, CA: Stanford University Press, 1993), pp. 98–126.

[2] For detailed accounts of the emergence of today's Russian Federation, see Gail W. Lapidus and Edward W. Walker, 'Nationalism, Regionalism and Federalism: Center–Periphery Relations in Post-Communist Russia', in Gail W. Lapidus (ed.), *The New Russia: Troubled Transformation* (Boulder, CO: Westview Press, 1995), pp. 79–113; and Elizabeth Teague, 'Center–Periphery Relations in the Russian Federation', in Roman Szporluk (ed.), *National Identity and Ethnicity in Russia and the New States of Eurasia* (Armonk, NY: M. E. Sharpe, 1994), pp. 21–57.

[3] Nail Midkhatovich Moukhariamov, 'The Tatarstan Model: A Situational Dynamic', in Peter J. Stavrakis *et al.* (eds), *Beyond the Monolith: The Emergence of Regionalism in Post-Soviet Russia* (Washington DC: Woodrow Wilson Center Press, 1997), p. 216.

[4] Article 61 of the Tatarstan constitution reads: 'The Republic of Tatarstan is a sovereign state, a subject of international law, associated with the Russian Federation and Russia on the basis of an Agreement on the reciprocal delegating of plenary powers and subjects of authority'; Moukhariamov, 'The Tatarstan Model', p. 219.

[5] M. N. Guboglo (ed.), *Federalism Vlasti i Vlast Federalisma* (Moscow: TOO 'IntelTekh', 1997), p. 247.

[6] Russian Minister of Finance Mikhail Zadornov, interviewed in *Argumenty i Fakty*, 16 February 1999, in *BBC Summary of World Broadcasts, The Former Soviet Union* (SWB/SU) 3463 B/7, 19 February 1999.

[7] Stig Kjeldsen, *The Treaty Process Evolves – Russian Bilateral Power-Sharing Treaties*, unpublished paper, School of Slavonic and East European Studies, University of London, 1999.

Chapter 2

[1] L. V. Smirnyagin, *Rossiiskii Federalizm: Paradoksy, Protivorechiya, Predrassudki* (Moscow: Moskovskii Obshchestvennyi Nauchnyi Fond, 1998), pp. 22–23.
[2] 'Ekspert Publishes New Regional Rankings', EastWest Institute, *Russian Regional Report*, vol. 3, no. 42, 22 October 1998.
[3] 'Kuda by Stolitsu Perenesti?', *Kommersant Vlast*, no. 17, 5 May 1999, pp. 4–5.
[4] *Human Development Report 1998, Russian Federation* (Moscow: UN Development Programme, 1998), pp. 77–78.
[5] Stephanie Harter, *From 'Third Rome' to 'Third Italy'? Economic Networks in Russia*, Research Paper in Russian and East European Studies 97/1 (Birmingham, UK: University of Birmingham Centre for Russian and East European Studies, 1997), p. 11.
[6] Archie Brown *et al.* (eds), *The Cambridge Encyclopaedia of Russia and the Soviet Union* (Cambridge: Cambridge University Press, 1982), p. 336.
[7] Olga Kryshtanovskaya and Stephen White, 'From Soviet Nomenklatura to Russian Elite', *Europe–Asia Studies*, vol. 48, no. 5, 1996, p. 728.
[8] Robert McIntyre, 'Regional Stabilisation Policy under Transition Period Conditions in Russia: Price Controls, Regional Trade Barriers and Other Local-Level Measures', *Europe–Asia Studies*, vol. 50, no. 5, 1998, p. 861.
[9] Andrei Bagrov, 'Komandy "Volno!" ne Bylo', *Kommersant Vlast*, 15 September 1998, p. 17.
[10] Natan Shklyar, 'Economic Crisis Strengthens Governors', *Russian Regional Report*, vol. 4, no. 1, 14 January 1999.
[11] Peter Kirkow, *Russia's Provinces: Authoritarian Transformation versus Local Autonomy?* (London: Macmillan, 1998), p. 115.
[12] A. M. Lavrov, 'Nekotorye Problemy Mezhbyudzhetnykh Otnoshenii v Rossii', paper delivered at the Economic and Social Research Council (ESRC) seminar 'Regional Transformations in the Russian Federation', Birmingham University, UK, 20 May 1998.
[13] 'UES: Between a Gloomy Present and a Brighter Future', *Emerging Markets Investment Research*, 8 December 1997, p. 2.
[14] 'Pool Power: Transforming Russia's Electric Utilities', *ibid.*, 13 August 1997, p. 7.
[15] 'Regions Fail to Cover Bonds', *Russian Regional Report*, vol. 3, no. 23, 11 June 1998.
[16] Aleksandr Golubev and Yulia Papilova, 'Krasnoyarskaya Korrida', *Kommersant Vlast*, 16 February 1999, p. 21.
[17] The 13 'donor' regions are: the republics of Tatarstan and Bashkortostan; St Petersburg; Moscow city and *oblast*; Khanty-Mansy and Yamal-Nenets autonomous *okrugs*; Krasnoyarsk Krai; and Irkutsk, Lipetsk, Perm, Samara and Sverdlovsk *oblasts*. See 'Who Are the Donor Regions?', *Russian Regional Report*, vol. 4, no. 20, 27 May 1999.
[18] Laura Solanko, 'Issues in Intergovernmental Fiscal Relations: Possible Lesson for Economies in Transition', *Review of Economies in Transition*, Bank of Finland, no. 5, 27 November 1998, p. 8.

Chapter 3

[1] Jeffrey W. Hahn, 'Regional Elections and Political Stability in

Russia', *Post-Soviet Geography and Economics*, vol. 38, no. 5, January 1997, pp. 252–53.

[2] 'Two Suspects Confess to Murdering Journalist', RFE/RL Newsline, 16 June 1998.

[3] 'Lebed Signs Agreement Allowing Moscow to Take Over Local TV Station', *Russian Regional Report*, vol. 4, no. 6, 18 February 1999.

[4] 'Primorsky Krai Governor Consolidates Hold over Media', *ibid.*, vol. 3, no. 48, 3 December 1998.

[5] Viktor Banev, 'Bashkirskii Variant Prezidentskoi Isbiratelnoi Kampanii', *Nezavisimaya Gazeta*, 17 June 1998.

[6] Radio Russia, 24 April 1999, in SWB/SU 3518 B/9, 26 April 1999.

[7] 'Resolution of 24 January 1997 on the Constitutionality of the Law of the Udmurt Republic of 17 April 1996 "On the System of Organs of State in the Udmurt Republic"', *Vestnik Konstitutsionnogo Suda Rossiiskoi Federatsii*, no. 1, 1997.

[8] 'Resolution of 4 April 1996 on the Constitutionality of a Number of Normative Acts of the City of Moscow and Moscow Oblast, Stavropol Krai, Voronezh Oblast and Voronezh City Regulating the Procedure for Registering Citizens for Permanent Residence in the Named Regions', *ibid.*, no. 2, 1996.

[9] Federal News Service, Moscow, 26 January 1999, in SWB/SU 3443 B/5–7, 27 January 1999.

Chapter 4

[1] Neil Melvin, *Regional Foreign Policies in the Russian Federation* (London: Royal Institute of International Affairs (RIIA), 1995), p. 17.

[2] ITAR-TASS, 29 June 1999, in SWB/SU 3576 B/6, 2 July 1999.

[3] Natan Shklyar, 'Economic Crisis Strengthens Governors', *Russian Regional Report*, vol. 4, no. 1, 14 January 1999.

[4] Eduard Kuzmin, 'Russia: The Center, the Regions, and the Outside World', *International Affairs* (Moscow), vol. 45, no. 1, 1999, pp. 118–19.

[5] Statement by Russian Minister of Nationalities Ramazan Abdulatipov at the signing ceremony of a five-year inter-regional cooperation agreement between Russia's Voronezh Oblast and Luhansk Oblast in Ukraine, 24 February 1999. See Andrei Muchnik, 'Voronezh, Ukrainian Region Sign Cross-border Treaty', *Russian Regional Report*, vol. 4, no. 9, 11 March 1999.

[6] Radio Russia, 12 April 1999, in SWB/SU O585 WA/13, 23 April 1999.

[7] For detailed accounts of the causes and effects of the Chechen war, see Carlotta Gall and Thomas de Waal, *Chechnya: A Small Victorious War* (London: Pan Books, 1997); and Anatol Lieven, *Chechnya: Tombstone of Russian Power* (New Haven, CT and London: Yale University Press, 1998).

[8] Interview with Georgian Minister of State Vazha Lortkipanidze, *Rezonansi*, 10–11 February 1999, in SWB/SU 3461 F/3, 17 February 1999.

[9] Gilbert Rozman, 'The Crisis of the Russian Far East: Who Is to Blame?', *Problems of Post-Communism*, vol. 44, no. 5, September–October 1997, p. 5.

[10] James Clay Moltz, 'Core and Periphery in the Evolving Russian Economy: Integration or Isolation of the Far East?', *Post-Soviet Geography and Economics*, vol. 37, no. 3, March 1996, p. 190.

[11] Michael Bradshaw, *The Russian*

Far East: Prospects for the New Millennium (London: RIIA, 1999), p. 28.

12 *Ibid.*, p. 9.

13 *Ibid.*, p. 29.

14 Yevgenii Popravko, 'Presidents Sign Agreement on Nakhodka', *Russian Regional Investor*, vol. 1, no. 21, 3 June 1999.

15 Alexander Lukin, 'The Image of China in Russian Border Regions', *Asian Survey*, vol. 38, no. 9, September 1998, pp. 822–23.

16 Bradshaw, *The Russian Far East*, p. 13.

17 'Seleznev Compares Illegal Influx of Chinese with "Territorial Expansion"', ITAR-TASS, 26 June 1998, in SWB/SU 3265 B/11, 29 June 1998.

18 Dmitri Trenin, *Kitaiskaya Problema Rossii* (Moscow: Carnegie Center, 1998), p. 42.

19 'Joint Declaration Gives Impetus to Peace Treaty Talks', Interfax, 13 November 1998, in SWB/SU 3384 B/13, 14 November 1998.

20 David S. Yost, *The US and Nuclear Deterrence in Europe*, Adelphi Paper 326 (Oxford: Oxford University Press for the IISS, 1999), p. 22.

21 *The Military Balance 1998/99* (Oxford: Oxford University Press for the IISS, 1998), p. 113.

22 *The Military Balance 1992/93* (London: Brassey's for the IISS, 1992), p. 98.

23 *Rossiiskie Regiony posle Vyborov – 96* (Moscow: Yuridicheskaya Literatura, 1997), p. 99.

24 'Ministry of Foreign Affairs Concerned about Governors' Foreign Activities', *Russian Regional Report*, vol. 3, no. 23, 11 June 1998.

25 Kuzmin, 'Russia', p. 113.

26 Nikolai Petrov, 'A Tale of Two Referenda', *Prism*, vol. 4, no. 10, 15 May 1998.

27 'On Co-ordination of International and External Economic Relations of the Constituent Entities of the Russian Federation', adopted by the State Duma on 2 December 1998 and signed into law by Yeltsin on 4 January 1999.

28 *Economic Survey: Russian Federation 1997* (Paris: Organisation for Economic Cooperation and Development (OECD), 1998), pp. 192–97.

29 *The Military Balance 1998/99*, p. 105.

30 Yuri Rodygin, 'Military Faces Tough Times in Volga Region', *Russian Regional Report*, vol. 3, no. 23, 11 June 1998.

31 Interview with Viktor Ishaev, *Izvestiya*, 5 March 1998, p. 4.

32 Interview with Mikhail Pogosyan, General Director, Sukhoi Military Industrial Group, Interfax, 12 January 1999, in SWB/SUW 0573 WA/11, 29 January 1999.

33 ITAR-TASS News Agency, 26 January 1999.

34 See, for example, Moscow Oblast's report on its assistance with the 1998 draft. Yevgenii Lisanov, 'Armiya i Mestnaya Vlast: o Schluzbe Zabota Obshchaya', *Krasnaya Zvezda*, 11 June 1998, p. 1.

35 *The Military Balance 1998/99*, p. 270.

36 Interview with Tatarstan President Mintimer Shaimiev, *Krasnaya Zvezda*, 11 April 1998.

37 See, for example, 'Gubernator – eto Dolzhnost dlya Bitiya', *Izvestiya*, 28 February 1999, p. 3.

38 'Federal Non-payments Cause Energy Crisis in Sakhalin Region', Nesavisimoye Televidenie, 18 April 1999, in SWB/SU 3513 B/9, 20 April 1999.

39 Press Service of the Karelian Prime Minister, 9 September 1998, www.gov.karelia.ru/gov/News/Leader/1998/0916_a.html.

40 *Izvestiya*, 6 August 1998, p. 2.

[41] Yulia Yeliseeva, 'Ayatskov Tries Out Role of Nuclear Extremist', *Russian Regional Report*, vol. 4, no. 12, 1 April 1999.
[42] See 'Russia's Desperate Military', *Strategic Comments*, vol. 4, no. 9, November 1998.

Conclusion

[1] See Ian Bremmer and Alyson Bailes, 'Sub-Regionalism in the Newly Independent States', *International Affairs*, vol. 74, no. 1, January 1998, p. 145.